Carpet
and Textile
Patterns

Carpet and Textile Patterns

by Nicholas Purdon

Flowers

Medallions

Stripes

Palmettes

Trees and Leaves

Compartments and Lattices

Niches

Figurative Motifs and Patterns

Stars

Abstract Shapes and Symbols

Octagons and Güls

Border and Guard Patterns

Published 1996 by Laurence King Publishing
an imprint of Calmann & King Ltd
71 Great Russell Street
London
WC1B 3BN

A catalogue record for this book is
available from the British Library.

ISBN 1 85669 081 4

Designed by Misha and Helen Anikst
Picture research by Andy Daniels
Printed in Hong Kong

Introduction

 Few media exemplify such a cornucopia of patterns and designs as are found in the textile arts. This is unsurprising, if one considers the universality of this art form, which eloquently expresses the design vocabulary of many disparate, if inter-related, cultures.

A brief look through this book should be sufficient to grasp the diversity of textile patterns. Weavings from England, France, the Balkans, Turkey, Persia, India, Southeast Asia and the Americas are all included. Designs range from the ornate and curvilinear examples of court ateliers or royal workshops to the tribal weavings of the nomad's loom, striking in their simplicity. The selection is by no means impartial, however. Following the author's own predilections, the vast majority of examples are Asian; further, a disproportionate number of pieces are woven in knotted pile. Despite this, the variety displayed defies easy categorisation.

Carpet enthusiasts often quote Paul Gauguin's comment: 'Oh, you painters who ask for a technique of colour – study carpets and there you will find all knowledge'. One could just as legitimately tell artists in any medium that the study of carpet and textile designs will provide an infinite source of inspiration. Such is the purpose of this book. By giving the reader an overview of over 270 examples of woven art, it is hoped that he or she will understand something of what it is for patterns and designs to be successful. It would, nevertheless, be disingenuous to suggest that the book does not seek to proselytise: it is hoped that the illustrated textiles will whet the reader's appetite, and excite curiosity in a medium too often regarded as inaccessible or rarefied.

The book is divided thematically into twelve chapters, each devoted to a particular theme. Short introductions discuss the illustrated examples, drawing parallels and pointing out stylistic quirks, while at the same time explaining the significance of particular patterns or motifs to textile art. So, the chapter entitled *Niches* not only compares and contrasts the numerous styles of niche, it also contains a brief exegesis on the importance of the shape in the Islamic world. *Flowers* looks at both representational and abstract depictions of floral forms, and considers this dichotomy in other media. In each chapter, an attempt has been made to keep a balance between different weaving cultures, but this has often been impossible. Particular traditions often favour particular styles, hence the preponderance of Caucasian pieces in *Stripes*, for example.

The majority of the text has been devoted to captions. Each example (robe, rug, sari etc) is given a standard geographical and tribal attribution together with a date. The newcomer to textile art will find some of these confusing, especially if he or she is unfamiliar with the cultural context in which these pieces were made. Carpets and textiles are broadly speaking classified thus: object, town or village in which weaving is produced (if known) or an ethnographic attribution (if known), country of origin, date. The beginner would do well simply to concentrate on the date and the country of origin – from this information alone much can be gleaned about cultural and historical trends. Rather than doing away with other details, however, these have been included in the hope that an interest to delve further into certain weavings will not be thwarted by a dearth of information.

Primarily, the captions set out to analyse different patterns or motifs, drawing attention to techniques, materials, colours and styles. They also provide supplementary points of interest. To some extent the book's title is a misnomer, for it is not just a study of *patterns*. Often the emphasis is on specific ornaments or motifs – the essential building blocks of patterns. Attempts have been made to place the pieces in the context of the culture which produced them and to examine the design origins of particular patterns. Finally, comparisons are drawn with other examples in the book. This book in no way claims to be a definitive account; its interpretations are all open to question. Indeed, very often a successful pattern is one which defies neat categorisation. Though clearly defined groups do exist (for example, *botehs* in *Trees and Leaves*), it is almost impossible to impose any kind of consistent and coherent order throughout.

I am indebted to all those who suffered my choleric temperament during the months in which this book was written – too many to mention. Specifically, I would like to thank Philip Cooper and Mary Scott at Laurence King for their painstaking editing of the text, and Misha and Helen Anikst for the design. Robert Pinner's cantankerous advice throughout the project was invaluable. I am grateful to Michael Franses for his fine-tuning of many of my attributions of the illustrated examples. Thanks also to Alan Marcuson for providing me with the idea and opportunity to write the book, and to my father for providing me with many good transparencies of wonderful pieces. My most particular thanks, however, goes to Andy Daniels, who carefully monitored the pictures and intelligently liaised with institutions on my behalf; his efficiency was all the more startling in the light of his wilful determination to show no interest in the book's subject whatsoever.

Flowers

The flower has inspired designs in every medium, each vastly different in conception and purpose. There are numerous reasons for the popularity of floral designs in art, but it is clear that flowers are attractive for their colour, their symbolism and their capacity to convey feelings of opulence and luxury.

In art, floral designs range from the minimal stylised renditions on the Geometric vase paintings of the Greeks to the naturalistic depictions on Dutch (and other) paintings (and embroideries) in the 17th and 18th centuries. The notable Dutch flower painter Jan van Huysum (1682-1749), insisted on painting from nature itself, often waiting until the next season to procure fresh blooms for the completion of his composition. Similarly, floral depictions on weaving from the famous Savonnerie manufactory also set about to imitate rather than interpret nature (*Plate 14*).

However, in carpet and textile art we often encounter more abstract and stylised floral forms. Often, indeed, flowers serve as an inspiration for a host of patterns which, at first sight, do not appear 'floral' at all (see, for example, *Plate 17*). The term '*gül*' is used to describe many rug ornaments which bear little relation to their floral origins (see *Octagons and Güls*). The disc-shaped rosettes of *Plates 16* and *18* are similarly interpretative, forming powerful abstract designs.

This chapter contains numerous floral patterns from the Indian tradition, characterised by an unparalleled attention to detail (*Plates 1, 2, 3, 7, 9* and *10*). This is exemplified by the delicate versions of the 'shrub' shown here (*Plates 1* and *3*), an element that was assimilated and adapted by numerous weaving traditions (*Plates 5, 6* and *8*).

In contrast, we often see less detailed workings of the flower, the emphasis being placed on the creation of a decorative pattern rather than on a precisely drawn ornament. So, on the 'Mina Khani' design of *Plates 21* and *22* the whole pattern takes precedence over its many constituent elements; if undue attention were given to specific flowers, the pattern would lose its balance and thus its power. On *Plate 4*, the simplified shrubs are de-emphasised in favour of the attractive latticework pattern. The commercial demands of Europe undoubtedly exerted an influence on the weaver's repertoire of floral designs. It has been suggested that St Petersburg decorators began the trend by commissioning floral carpets in a Western tradition from their Caucasian suppliers (see *Plate 12*) to complement Empire-style furniture, and Savonnerie designs are not uncommon on Caucasian rugs from Karabagh and on northwest Persian decorative carpets (*Plate 13*). However, there was probably also a cross-cultural exchange of ideas before this rapid commercialisation of Near Eastern weaving.

1 *Mughal carpet, India (detail)*
second quarter 17th century
Shrubs are common motifs on many Indian carpets, comprising diverse flowerheads growing out of stems with realistically drawn serrated leaves. The attention to detail is extraordinary. During the reign of Jahangir (r. 1605-27), trade with the West brought European botanical paintings to India, which inspired Mughal artists to reproduce their own plants naturalistically.

2 *Mughal rug, India (detail)*
first half 17th century
The flowerheads on this superb rug fall within a trellis formed by curved serrated leaves and are not unlike the sunflower motif at the centre of *Plate 7*. The fineness of the weave on such 'classical' Indian pieces gives them an intricacy and verisimilitude not often found on knotted carpets. Flowers depicted as seen from above are common throughout the textile arts and are sometimes called rosettes.

Flowers

3 *North Indian* qanat *(tent hanging)*

18th century

This stamped and painted shrub is more simply drawn in outline, although its flowerhead is delineated by multiple fine brown-black lines; it would be difficult to achieve such an effect on pile (or flatwoven) pieces.

4 *Afshar rug, Kirman Province, South Persia*

19th century

An all-over shrub design has been employed here. More Oriental style flowerheads sit on cruciform stems within a red-pink twig lattice.

5 *Qashqa'i rug, Southwest Persia (detail)*

dated 1334 AH (AD 1915)

Two different sets of shrubs, one large and drawn perspectively, the other small and simple, are set diagonally on an emerald green ground.

6 *Ottoman* bohça, *Turkey (detail)*

17th or 18th century

These shrubs have the same form as those in *Plates 1* and *3*, but the leaves have more fluid and uniform curves while the carnation-like flowerheads themselves are stylised.

7 *Kashmir shawl, India*

18th century

Shrubs are apparent within the compartments of this brilliant shawl, although they are more stylised than those in *Plates 1* and *3*. Most impressive, however, are the radiant flowerheads within the medallion, especially the sunflower at the centre. Shawls with a medallion and corner format are rare and highly valued.

3

4

5

6

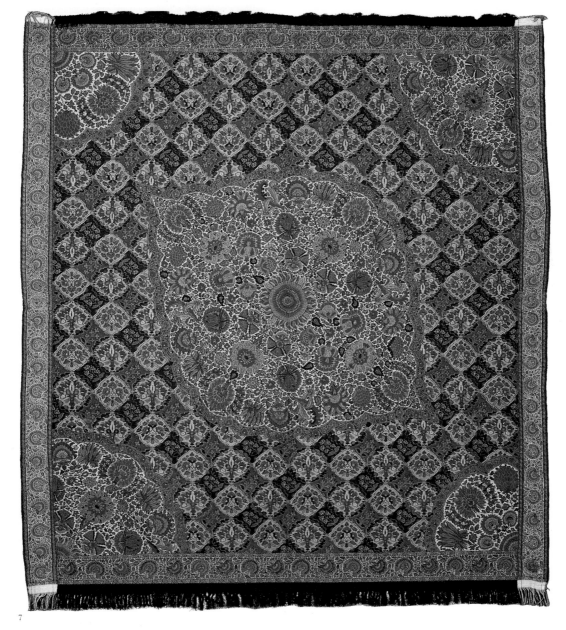

7

Flowers

8 Khotan carpet, East Turkestan

19th century

Medium-sized rounded flower-heads or rosettes grow in sets of five out of a creeper lattice in which *fleur-de-lis* designs and larger generic flowers are also set. This profusion of simple flowers, set among a green lattice, owes much to the Indian 'millefleurs' pattern (*Plates 9* and *10*) in conception. The shrubs in the border have flowerheads of great originality and diversity. They perhaps owe something to shrubs found on Indian pieces, as seen in *Plates 1* and *3*.

9 Kashmir (?) rug, India

late 17th or early 18th century
Carpets with this pattern are known as 'millefleurs' (see also *Plate 10*). As the name suggests, thousand of flowerheads of subtly different types are carefully ordered to create a distinctive pattern. Often the 'millefleurs' pattern is rendered in a prayer format with a niche superimposed. Here, the majority of the flowers grow out of a single vase, making the pattern more directional. The pattern is less uniform than in *Plate 10*, criss-crossing tendrils, half-cypress trees and the niche all serving to break up the design.

10 Mughal carpet, probably Lahore, North India (detail)

second half 18th century
This carpet bears a typical 'mille-fleurs' pattern. The design is derived from that of Mughal lattice carpets (e.g. *Plate 2*) and bears a close resemblance to *Comp-artments and Lattices, Plate 15* in conception.

8

9

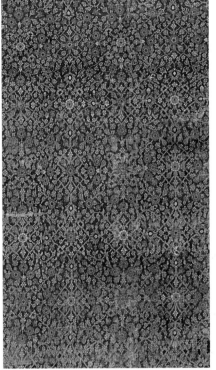

10

Flowers

11 Scane flatweave, Scandinavia

c.1800

An array of flowers, some realistic, others naive form a wreath around the horseman, possibly a Magus.

12 Zeikhur rug, Northeast Caucasus (detail)

19th century

These rose flowerheads are alternated with 'cauliflowers', each depicted primarily in two colours to give them a three-dimensionality. The design certainly owes much to Western traditions of decoration; yet the rug itself need not be a commercial product made for immediate export; it could equally be a hybrid, representing the cultural exchange of decorative motifs

13 Bijar carpet, Northwest Persia (detail)

late 19th century

Bouquets of three realistically drawn roses are framed by rococo cartouches. The carpet nicely exemplifies the cultural exchange of designs between the Near East and the West. The floriate field owes a great deal to the designs in *Plate 14*.

14 Louis XIV Savonnerie carpet, France (detail)

mid 17th century

The flowers on this carpet bring to mind naturalistic, still-life depictions in Dutch painting. Such renditions were to prove the benchmark for all successive Western decorative traditions and also appealed to the weaving traditions of Asia. The overall effect is one of abundance and wealth – appropriate enough when one considers the luxurious buildings for which many of these carpets were intended. True Savonneries were made only in the manufactory commissioned by Louis XIII in 1644 – La Savonnerie ('soap factory') – on a site corresponding to the present-day Musée d'Art Moderne in Paris.

15 Afshar rug, Kirman Province (detail)

19th century

Occidentalising designs are common to many weaving cultures in the 19th century. The *gol farang* (*farang* literally means 'from France', but came to denote 'European') design on this Afshar takes French-style designs as its starting point and adapts them. Sumptuous bouquets of rose-like flowerheads among realistically drawn leaves are woven in diagonals on a white field divided into compartments by columns of smaller red flowerheads.

11

12

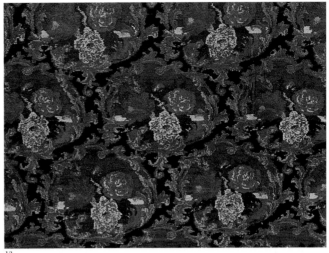

13

14

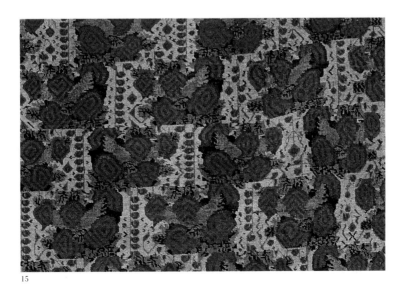

15

Flowers

16 Bukhara suzani, Uzbekistan (detail)
19th century
These beautiful, disc shaped rosettes, taken from the border, are given three-dimensionality through the layering of different shapes within the whole.

17 Kuba rug, Northeast Caucasus
19th century
The flowerheads on this typical Kuba district weaving are highly abstract rosettes. However, the serrated outline of each ornament, and the colours in which each has been woven evoke petals; while the star-filled diamonds within perhaps represent each open flower's stamen. The 'leaf and wineglass' border can be seen used on *Border and Guard Patterns, Plate 8*.

18 Ottoman embroidery, Turkey (detail)
18th century
A rosette surrounded by a circular snake in yellow and beige (perhaps a stylised rendition of the calyx) comes alive through the use of six different layers of contrasting colours. The navy blue leaf shapes recall bunches of grapes, also found on Ottoman embroideries. The field is strewn with fuschia coloured 'daisies' and azure blue tulips.

19 Kashan (?) carpet, Central Persia (detail)
20th century
Brilliant white six-petalled rosettes stand out sharply from a shaded indigo field; the design and colouring are perhaps inspired by Chinese patterns, and the piece's uniformity is quite effective.

16

17

18

19

Flowers

20 Kerman vase carpet, South-Central Persia (detail)

17th or early 18th century
'Vase' is a term used to describe carpets with a particular design and structure, although only two highly stylised 'vase' shapes (in green) are evident on this piece. Multi-directional flowerheads, blossoms and palmettes are set in abundance within a lattice on a claret ground. The pattern is successful largely as a result of the great diversity of its many floral ornaments.

21 Kurdish rug, Northwest Persia (detail)

19th century
The 'Mina Khani' design, commonly found on a variety of Northwest Persian weavings, usually comprises two types of major flowerhead ornaments, one daisy-like and set at the intersections of a trellis, the other more ragged and stylised, set within each compartment. White blossoms complete the pattern. This fine example has uniformity without appearing rigid. Its glowing colours, particularly the light blue of the ragged flowerheads, are particularly striking.

22 Baluch rug, Northeast Persia (detail)

18th or 19th century
As in *Plate 20*, a trellis has been superimposed on blossoms, daisies and ragged flowerheads. This unusual tribal rendition of the 'Mina Khani' design loses none of its character through being rectilinear nor through its more limited palette – the fine quality of wool makes the piece shine. Simple hound shapes throughout the field add further character. Rugs woven by the confederation of tribes known as Baluch commonly have such a red-blue palette.

23 Zeikhur long rug, Northeast Caucasus (detail)

mid 19th century
This piece owes much in conception, if not in execution to classical Persian vase carpets (e.g. *Plate 21*). On an almost scarlet ground, multiple stylised flowers and foliate forms appear in pinks, blues and greens, interspersed with figurative ornaments. The seemingly clumsy, rectilinear blue vases are themselves decorated with small flowers.

20

21

22

23

Palmettes

A palmette may be defined as an ornament 'with narrow divisions or digitations, somewhat resembling a palm leaf' (*Oxford English Dictionary*). However, even the most stylised palmettes clearly represent kinds of flowerhead, and they are often woven over leaves, stems or calyces, as in *Plates 6, 9, 10, 14* and *17*. What distinguishes palmettes from other floral motifs is that they seem to be flowerheads viewed at eye level. One sees the petals and leaves of the plant almost in cross-section. Rosettes, on the other hand, are open flowerheads as viewed from above. The palmette is most clearly expressed in the neat and simple versions found in *Plate 5*.

Palmettes are ubiquitous in carpet and textile traditions but are often used diversely and with great originality. Safavid court carpets (e.g. *Plates 1, 2*) include several varieties of palmette, all carefully delineated, often with one type woven inside another.

Some palmettes are jagged edged, as on *Plates 1, 2, 3* and *10*. On many of these the digitations that help characterise the palmette are absent; instead the palmette is filled with further palmettes (*Plates 2* and *3*) or with floral forms (*Plate 10*). The palmettes in *Plate 7* have similarly serrated edges and achieve a certain three-dimensionality from the layering of many different segments (an effect also seen in *Plate 18*). Sometimes digitations actually leave the palmette and protrude into the field, as on the *harshang* motif of *Plate 4* and in *Plate 9*, thereby creating a more pronounced, ragged outline.

Countless Ottoman weavings use tulips and other floral ornaments in cross-section. The carnations in *Plate 14* consist merely of seven simply drawn segments. The 'bear's feet' in *Plate 8* and the comparable tulips in *Plate 12* and *15* likewise use a few simple shapes – here flowing lines in series – to create palmette-like motifs. The smooth-edged palmettes in *Plate 11* dispense with all such complexities, serving instead as blocks of colour for the embroidered flowers within.

In Caucasian weaving, palmettes become rectilinear (*Plate 18*) or stylised (*Plate 16*). Such motifs were used to form complex patterns which would be handed down from generation to generation almost unchanged. They appear the least floral of all palmettes, and seem to have been taken from other traditions not least for their attractive shape. The stylised palmettes in *Plate 17*, also a Caucasian product, similarly adapt the palmette shape to create shield-like motifs.

1

1 *Esfahan carpet, Central Persia*
c.1650
The palmettes here are as those in *Plate 2*, but are more rotund and simply drawn. The cloud-bands (see *Abstract Shapes and Symbols, Plates 1-6*) too are stiffer.

2 *Esfahan carpet, Central Persia (detail)*
early 17th century
A variety of palmettes can be found on this carpet, all finely drawn and clearly outlined. They typify many of the curvilinear features of so-called Safavid carpets (see *Medallions, Plate 2*). 'Shah Abbasi' is the term often used to describe the individual motifs on carpets of this and following periods, after Shah Abbas (r. 1588-1629) who set up a court factory in his new capital, Esfahan. Cloud-bands (see *Abstract Shapes and Symbols, Plates 1-6*) and scrolling stems (see *Trees and Leaves, Plate 15*) also appear on the rich red field.

Palmettes

3 *Medallion carpet, South Caucasus*

18th century
Kurdish weaving often employs classical themes while incorporating the bright colours and informal repertoire of many tribal textiles. Around classical palmettes with bite-shaped edges (prototypes to which can be seen in *Plates 1* and *2*) and an austere lobed medallion are strewn the less formal ornaments and stylised figures found on many tribal rugs.

4 *Kuba carpet, East Caucasus (detail)*

17th or 18th century
The so-called *harshang* or 'crab' design comprises crab-like palmettes which form a central column and are framed by palmette-filled, jagged-edged flowerheads, here in dark blue and yellow. On a rose ground, the motifs of this carpet are so clearly drawn that they could almost have been printed, despite the gentle abrash which runs throughout the piece. Note also the ragged flowerheads used to break up the *harshang* palmettes of the central column and the tiny blossoms used as fillers throughout the field. Both, interestingly, have close counterparts in the example in *Plate 5*.

5 *Carpet fragment, Khorasan Province, Northeast Persia*

17th century
Palmettes are set like stamens within gracefully drawn petals. This wonderful pattern, while relying on the palmette designs of Safavid court carpets (for which see *Medallions, Plate 2*) has great originality. The palmettes themselves have been reduced to their barest components, like those which fill the *harshang* motifs in *Plate 4*. Note also the reciprocal trefoils of the main border and outer guard (see *Border and Guard Patterns, Plate 17*) – the blue and yellow colour combination on the latter is reproduced on some 'Polonaise' carpets.

3

4

5

Palmettes

6 Beshir carpet, Turkmenistan (detail)

18th or 19th century

The grand palmettes employed on this carpet evoke a British coat-of-arms. Their distinctly regal feel has led some to suggest that this was a palace carpet woven specially for the Emir of Bukhara. Again the palmettes grow out of roots and leaves, which in this instance call to mind the motifs of the much-used *herati* design (see *Trees and Leaves, Plate 8*).

7 West Anatolian rug, Turkey

17th century

This rug is of the so-called Smyrna design, named after the West Anatolian town (now Izmir) where such carpets were once thought to be made. Complex palmettes made up of layered contrasting shapes in red, yellow, orange, blue and beige are ringed by red sprays on an *abrashed* green ground.

8-11 Four Ottoman embroideries, Turkey (details)

16th–18th centuries

A multitude of embroideries were made in Ottoman households for a variety of uses, including bedspreads. They are replete with motifs, most notably palmettes of great diversity. In *Plate 8* red 'bear's feet' (perhaps tulips) are alternated with blue palmettes; both have simple round pink flowerheads for calyces. *Plates 9* and *10* show more jagged versions of palmette. On the latter, each individual petal-like digitation has been embroidered separately, so that it may also be read as an open flowerhead. Those of the former are less segmented and are filled with Ottoman tulips (see *Plates 12* and *15*) and other floral elements. They perhaps call to mind Ottoman carnations (see *Plate 14*). Both are embraced by blue leaves, making each design unit comparable to either a shrub (see *Flowers, Plates 1, 3* and *5-8*) or a flower and calyx. The palmettes in *Plate 11*, which appear within a red diamond lattice, are smooth-edged and appear distended. These too are embellished with simple leaves, and with flowers typically Ottoman in style. While all these ornaments are clearly floral, they have been classified as palmettes because they appear as viewed from eye-level.

6

7

8

9

10

11

Palmettes

12 Ottoman short-sleeved kaftan, Turkey
16th or 17th century
Crescents and tulips – whose curved outer sections bring to mind the large petals in *Plate 5* – are executed in appliqué on crimson satin. This technique gives a design of great clarity. The 'balls' at each tulip's root strongly bring to mind the so-called *çintamani* design (see *Abstract Shapes and Symbols, Plates 17-19*).

13 Afshar bag-face, Kirman Province, South Persia
19th century
This representation of tulips is common on tribal pilewoven products from Kirman. They are not unlike pineapples in appearance.

14 Ottoman velvet, Turkey (detail)
16th century
Silver-white carnations, each made up by seven slices, are brocaded onto a burgundy ground to give a design of great clarity. Indeed, the success of the pattern derives from its rigid simplicity. The palmette proper grows out of a stylised root with leaves.

15 Iznik tile, Turkey
17th or 18th century
These tulips are made up of three simple wavy blue lines and bear comparison with those in *Plate 12*. They are also like the 'bear's feet' palmettes in *Plate 8*, but are more formal and flow more gracefully – perhaps a result of having been painted rather than woven.

12

13

14

15

Palmettes

16 Zeikhur rug, Northeast Caucasus

dated 1297 AH (AD 1879)
The design of this rug is named
the Bijov after the village in which
many pieces with this pattern were
supposedly made. Three columns
are formed by interconnected palmettes of several different forms.
In parts the blue-ground field is
broken up by lighter blue zigzags
(see also the field of *Medallions*,
Plate 13).

17 Shield carpet, Caucasus

18th century
'Shields' woven in turquoise, fawn,
green and red are repeated over a
blue ground with strong abrash.
Curled leaves (see *Trees and
Leaves, Plate 4*) at their base are
echoed in the border. Each shield
contains three very simply executed tree-like motifs and is framed
by pairs of white serrated leaves.

18 Kuba rug, East Caucasus (detail)

late 19th century
Such multilayered rectilinear palmettes are common on weaving of
the Eastern Caucasus. A three-
dimensional effect is created by
the contrasting colours on each
segment of the palmette. A similar
technique is used on the very different palmettes of *Plate 7*. The
pattern's success, however, is in its
unashamed use of bold colours for
each palmette; this is enhanced by
the natural wool ground colour.

19 Anatolian carpet, probably East Turkey (detail)

18th century
Blossoms and 'vine-leaf' palmettes
are set in a lattice, within which
are woven stars and rosettes. These
palmettes are thought to derive
from motifs found on some contemporaneous 'Classical' carpets
of the nearby southern Caucasus.

16

17

18

19

Trees and Leaves

Leaves and Composite Patterns

James Morton, who worked for a firm producing textiles and carpets in Ireland at the turn of the century, spoke of William Morris's designs having 'a suggestiveness of green meadows and many-coloured flowers, of waving trees and singing birds, and of as much beyond as one had power to read'. The same can be said of numerous patterns which combine arboreous and foliate elements to suggest dense growth and wild abundance.

Plate 1 shows oversized curled leaves in its field, growing in every direction. Interspersed with these and in the border is naturalistic foliage, conveying the impression of nature untamed. The leaves (and stylised brown tree) in *Plate 3*, although very different in conception, create a similar effect. The leafy patterns of both pieces provide a good backdrop for the assorted wildlife. The thick leaves in *Plate 2* also suggest abundance, although in a more ordered manner.

This chapter includes a number of composite patterns in which leaves are prominent amidst other floral and natural forms. By time-honoured convention, Persian and other weaving traditions have used scrolling stems and arabesques to connect assorted individual palmettes or other motifs (*Plates 17* and *18*). The use of scrolling stems and leaves to link numerous disparate motifs on carpets was adopted by the West, as can be seen on *Plates 20* and *21*, both English carpets. Sometimes arabesques become so abstracted that their relation to foliate forms becomes tenuous (*Plates 15, 16* and *19*).

Leaves can be rendered in an ordered fashion either as motifs repeated in an all-over pattern, or as field decoration around a medallion (*Plates 5* and *8*). The leaves in *Plate 7* and the *herati* design of *Plate 8* both use groups of four leaves curling away from a central diamond. The *boteh* design (*Plates 9-14*) is a good example of a leaf-like ornament used in an ordered repeat, although different traditions have *botehs* drawn with varying degrees of uniformity. Doubtless, such designs were the inspiration for 'paisley' patterns.

1 *'Feuilles de Choux au Cheval et la Lionne', possibly Enghien*
c.1550
The tapestries known as *Feuilles de Choux* ('Cabbage Leaves') or 'Large Leaf Verdure' comprise many sumptuous, verdant, large leaf designs, at once both realistic and stylised. They often contain, as here, fantastical birds and beasts, their overall composition bringing to mind the work of the Dutch painter Hieronymus Bosch (c.1450-1516), who probably in part inspired these designs.

2 *'The Fintona', Donegal carpet, Ireland (detail)*
c.1902
Oversized curvilinear leaves are distinguished from a green field, replete with numerous floral and tree forms, by thin white lines. Different outsized leaves in yellow and green frame the carpet. Carpets woven in County Donegal at the end of the 19th century and the beginning of the 20th include a wide variety of designs, many oriental, some – most notably those designed by C. F. A. Voysey (1857-1941) – in the Arts and Crafts mode. This design was probably woven for Liberty's.

1

Trees and Leaves

3 *Bakhshaish rug, West Persia*

19th century

This unusual rug contains many stylised leaves, growing out of the thin branches of a tree and simply drawn in many different colours. The comb shapes within the leaves are echoed in the feathers of the bird's tail. The tree itself comprises juxtaposed shapes divided into grids by thin brown lines in a way that suggests bark.

4 *Tekke* kapunuk, *Turkmenistan*

19th century

The 'curled leaf' design is found on a number of borders (see *Palmettes, Plate 17; Figurative Motifs and Patterns, Plate 16; Octagons and Güls, Plate 2; Border and Guard Patterns, Plate 19*), especially on Turkmen pieces. Each leaf's jagged edge recalls the ashik motif, also common on Turkmen weaving (see *Abstract Shapes and Symbols, Plate 24*), itself not unlike a leaf. The design is also found on a few 18th century Caucasian rugs (see *Palmettes, Plate 17*).

5 *George III Axminster carpet, England*

18th century

Large and scrolling leaves in the field intertwine and overlap in a manner reminiscent of arabesques (*Plates 15-19*), while still remaining firmly rooted in a European tradition. The skilful gradation of colour on these leaves gives a three-dimensional effect.

6 *Ottoman embroidery, Turkey (detail)*

17th century

Each leaf is crisply embroidered in blue and pink silk and combined with bear's feet (or tulip) flowerheads (see also *Palmettes, Plate 8*). The combination of rich dark blue with pink is very effective and characteristic of good Ottoman embroideries.

7 *Carpet fragment, Khorasan Province, Northeast Persia (detail)*

17th century

Four leaves are symmetrically placed around a diamond creeper, woven in orange. These 'sickle-leaf' motifs are arranged in a similar way to the leaves of the *herati* pattern (*Plate 8*), but curl in on each other more dramatically.

8 *South Persian carpet (detail)*

early 19th century

The so-called *herati* design is one of the most widespread of all Persianate patterns; it takes its name from the town of Herat, now in Afghanistan. Four 'fish-head' or leaf motifs are arranged around a diamond-shaped red-orange creeper; adjacent leaves from different design units scroll around a brown flowerhead. The formula would normally be repeated throughout the field to create an 'all-over' pattern. Here, however, a medallion and corner format has been imposed.

3

4

5

6

7

8

Trees and Leaves

Botehs

9 Sehna kilim, Northwest Persia (detail)

19th century

The origins of the highly enduring *boteh* pattern are a source of great debate. It has been compared to the impression caused by a closed fist on a mud or plaster surface, but is more likely, however, a representation of a leaf including its curled stalk (*boteh* is the Persian for a cluster of leaves). Every detail on these *botehs* (e.g. the flower-heads within each motif) is carefully rendered, creating a dense design which recalls the pine-cone. The overall effect is accentuated by the dark blue ground on which this pattern is often set.

10 Ottoman velvet, Turkey (detail)

18th century or earlier

The primary motifs on this attractive velvet are like *botehs* translated along their central axis and then reflected. They look like 'S' shapes or perching birds.

11 Shusha (?) brocade, West Caucasus (detail)

19th century

Here the *boteh* is rendered minimally, yet the pattern is made exciting through the varied use of colour. Each *boteh* is more clearly defined than on rugs or kilims, largely as a result of the weft-wrapping technique in which they are rendered, which allows for no grey area between a motif's outline and the field.

12 Beshir rug, Bukhara Emirate (detail)

18th/19th century

Here *botehs* are oversized and lack the decorative precision seen in *Plate 9*, for example. The pattern clearly made its way to central Asia, where it was to prove equally popular, also appearing on Ikat textiles woven in Uzbekistan (*Plate 13*).

13 Ikat panel, Uzbekistan (detail)

19th century

These elegantly curved botehs are simply drawn; complexities are ruled out by the difficult ikat technique. The pattern comes alive through the contrast of the yellow and white *botehs* with the pastel pink ground.

14 Khamseh rug, Southwest Persia (detail)

19th century

In this instance, smaller *botehs* grow in abundance out of the major ornament, creating a complex, more decorative effect, known as 'Mother and Child'. The innovation was adopted by the makers of shawls for the Western market in Kerman in Southern Persia and in Kashmir in India.

9

10

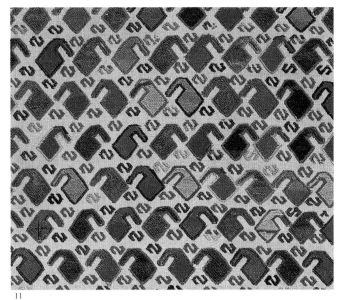

11

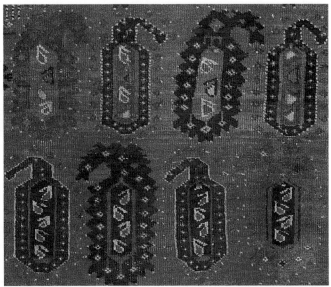

12

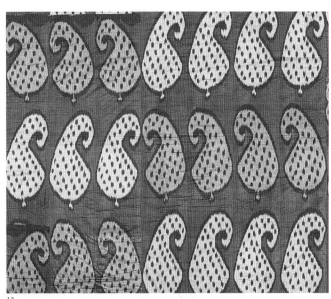

13

14

Trees and Leaves

Arabesques and Spiralling Stems

15 Iznik polychrome tile, Turkey

c.1570

Consisting primarily of split-leaf palmettes and other forms of stylised foliage connected by spiralling or undulating stems, the arabesque is one of the most enduring and widespread styles of decoration in near Eastern art. It is typified on this tile which shows its many and varied elements more clearly than a weaving.

16 Ottoman gown, Turkey

18th century

Angular arabesques are woven in silver thread on a dark blue ground. In style, these hark back to the early Ottoman or Seljuk period decoration. Such designs were to prove highly influential on European 'moresque' patterns, which frequently adapted the Islamic arabesque. The gown belonged to Fatma Sultan, a daughter of Mustafa III (r. 1757-74).

17 Esfahan carpet, Central Persia (detail)

early 17th century

These arabesques are all depicted as rough-edged leaves, naturalistically drawn and intertwined with cloudbands (see *Abstract Shapes and Symbols, Plates 1-6*). Despite the multi-directional pattern, the overall effect is quite restrained.

18 Silk and metal-thread Kum Kapı rug, Istanbul, Turkey (detail)

early 20th century

Both the red ground and the black border of this rug are filled with scrolling arabesques, with split-leaf palmettes partly woven in brilliant white silk. Rugs woven in the Kum Kapı district in Istanbul often have distinctive renderings of traditional classical designs, partly brought about through the fineness of the weave. Here, the deep madder niche outlined in gold owes much to its Ottoman predecessors (see *Niches, Plate 2*).

19 Bijar carpet, Northwest Persia (detail)

19th century

This carpet contains rectilinear white and light blue arabesques, each part of two separate creeper latticework systems.

15

16

17

18

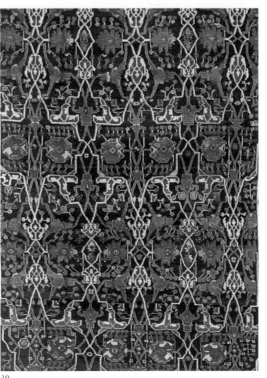

19

Trees and Leaves

20 *Morris & Co. Hammersmith carpet, England (detail)*
designed by William Morris in 1883
The 'Holland Park' design, of which this is an example, comprises orientalised palmettes and flowerheads shooting forth from scrolling leafy branches, woven in green and turquoise. The overall effect is one of abundance. The border was to prove influential on later Arts and Crafts carpets (see *Plate 2*).

21 *The Hulse carpet, probably England*
dated 1614
The concept of this pattern is oriental, with an abundance of flowers and fruit shooting forth from scrolling branches or stems. Both branches and leaves are variegated in yellows and greens to create a naturalistic effect. Worms, snakes, caterpillars and snails are also depicted.

20

Trees and Leaves

Trees

Trees in textile art embody a complex of ideas and symbols and often shun the wild abundance of foliate patterns. The cyprus tree (*Plates 22, 30 and 31*), for example, a common motif throughout the Islamic world, has great religious significance. Furthermore, the appearance of single trees within mihrabs (*Plates 24, 25 and 27*) perhaps harks back to a time when they were used as decoration for prayer rugs (see *Niches*, Introduction).

Many trees in textile art eschew naturalism, their abstract qualities possibly reflecting their symbolic value. So, *Plate 33* shows a simple trunk out of which grow stylised leaves whose colours and shape resemble little in nature. The trees in *Plates 27* and *28* avoid all complexity, the former using arrowheads, the latter latch-hooks in lieu of leaves. In *Plate 32* leaves are suggested by blue hooks, which are in many ways just a continuation of the trunk. Whatever the significance of such weavings, such tree patterns express concepts that are far distant from the naturalism of most leaf patterns.

Like scrolling stems, however, trees sometimes serve as a convenient platform for natural ornaments, and most especially leaves. Flora and fauna appear among the rectilinear branches in *Plate 26*. In the same way, the trees in *Plate 30* contain numerous small floral forms. The serpentine tree in *Plate 23*, while interesting in itself, is used as an armature for the numerous variegated leaves and flowers.

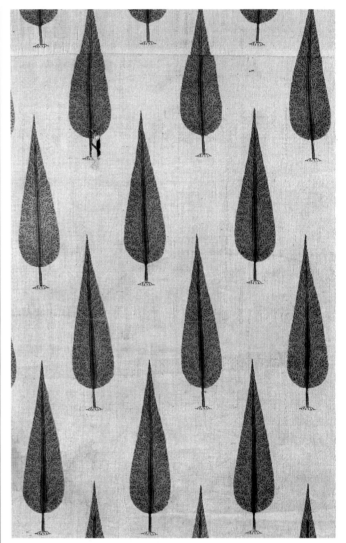

22

22 *Painted garment portion, Burhanpur, India (detail)*
18th century
Green cypress trees, inlaid with naturalistic branches, are repeated on a white ground in a way that is at once restrained and refined. The cypress tree is a holy tree and is a common motif throughout many textile and carpet traditions.

23 *Painted cotton (Chintz), South India*
18th century
Stylised serpent-like branches interlace and are embellished with sprays from which grow many different leaves with finely gradated colours; such detail would be difficult to reproduce on pile or flatwoven pieces, but is possible on painted fabrics.

23

Trees and Leaves

24 Baluch rug, Northeast Persia

19th century

This so-called 'Tree of Life', flanked by highly abstract tree forms, grows out of a 'barber's pole' trunk intersected by latch-hooks and diamond shapes. Out of these grow oversized serrated leaves, uniformly drawn in blue-green and brown. The tree itself grows into a rectangular niche; trees are often employed in prayer format rugs (see *Niches*, Introduction).

25 Thracian kilim

mid 19th century

Thracian kilims were made in the area which now includes western Turkey, eastern Greece and south-east Bulgaria. They are densely woven, and have clear colours and angular designs, often with trees. On this fine example, a green tree falls within a red niche. From gracefully drawn branches hang stylised flowerheads, picked up in the two large diamonds of the trunk. Delicately drawn thin leaves grow out of sprigs and are echoed outside the niche by 'wing' shapes.

26 Neriz rug, South Persia

second half 19th century

This is one of a well-known design group of yellow ground tree rugs, attributed to the town of Neriz. In the branches of a simply drawn, brown 'tree-of-life' are woven birds and flowers. Note also the use of *botehs* (see *Plates 9-14*) in the border.

27 Mudjur rug, Central Anatolia

early 19th century

Series of inward pointing arrow-heads in contrasting colours suggest dense foliage on this highly simpli-fied and abstract tree. The branch itself is made up of just a thin blue line intersected by small diamonds. Note how the angle of the branches corresponds to that of the stepped niche (see *Niches, Plate 13*). For the border, see *Border and Guard Patterns, Plate 14*.

28 Shirvan rug, East Caucasus

19th century

Repeated latch-hook (or animal head) chevrons create a stylised tree pattern complemented by a yellow ground floral border.

24

25

26

27

28

Trees and Leaves

29 *Brocaded panel, South Sumatra (detail)*
19th century
Purple branches scroll in towards a totemic trunk. The field is filled with stripes, chevrons and latch-hook motifs.

30 *Khorasan long rug, Northeast Persia (detail)*
first half 19th century
Cypress trees with uniform comb-like branches, and trees in blossom are interspersed with crosses and serrated half-diamonds. The blossoms are almost a working of the mina khani design in miniature (see *Flowers, Plates 20* and *21*).

31 *Bakhshaish carpet, West Persia (detail)*
19th century
The *bid majnun*, or weeping willow, design comprises the willow, cypress, poplar and fruit trees, all depicted in a simple, stylised manner. The fact that the design is wholly rectilinear perhaps indicates that such pieces belong to village and tribal traditions and were not the product of more commercial and sophisticated urban workshops.

32 *Yüncü kilim, Western Anatolia*
19th century
Drawn simply and rectilinearly in blue and red, the tree and leaf forms of this kilim have a decidedly contemporary feel. It is interesting to compare this trunk with that in *Plate 25*.

33 *Yomut* asmalyk, *Turkmenistan*
19th century
Soldat or 'tuning fork' strips (see also *Border and Guard Patterns, Plate 7*) serve as tree trunks and divide this *asmalyk* into compartments. Impressionistic leaves in orange, red, white, blue and brown complete these trees.

29

30

31

32

33

Compartments and Lattices

The compartment format is used on a wide variety of textiles, usually as a means of highlighting or framing design units. Compartments clearly announce the beginning of a new theme within an all-over design or simply underpin a single motif repeated throughout the field. They are often used in this way as frames for distinct elements. This is exemplified by the Bakhtiari Garden Rug (*Plate 2*) in which the numerous boxes that the superimposed grid creates contain a multiplicity of autonomous flower and tree patterns. It is not unlike looking at a cartoon strip, where each box signifies a different yet related event within the narrative. Grid compartments (i.e. those characterised by vertical and horizontal lines) are used in a similar way in *Plates 7* and *8*, where each compartment underpins a different block of colour. The compartments of *Plate 14*, likewise, encompass a diversity of floral designs.

Often compartments contain replicated or closely corresponding motifs in an all-over design. The repeated elephants in *Plate 4* are framed by a golden lattice; it is interesting to compare the effect created by *Figurative Motifs and Patterns, Plate 7*, where cows appear within an all-over design that is more stark for the absence of any imposed lattice. Compartments on Turkmen carpets are often explicitly used to enhance the primary *güls* (see *Octagons and Güls, Plate 2*). Similarly the compartments in *Plate 6*, the spray lattice in *Plate 10*, and the foliate lattice in *Plate 15* all enhance the motifs within them; the last of these considerably helps create the impression of diagonal bands of colour. The repeated square tiles of the Chessboard rug (*Plate 5*) suggest a grid lattice although none is actually explicit.

Part of the success of so-called 'Garden' carpet designs is perhaps that they embrace both uses of compartment structures. The waterways in *Plate 1* serve to highlight sections that are broadly the same (each a garden), while the smaller compartments frame different flowerbeds. Sometimes, however, lattices become primary decorative features. The thick, saw-shaped leaves in *Plate 16*, for example, are as important to the overall pattern as the palmettes and blossoms they contain. The brackets of the *aksu* design *Plate 13* appear primary, partly because of the way their natural colour stands out from the dark field. The brackets of the *Yün Tsai T'ou* design in *Plate 12* are the only field decoration – an ingenious use of a device usually employed to carry the main pattern.

1

1 'Garden' carpet, Northwest Persia (detail)

mid 18th century
Few patterns from Persian weaving traditions can be as engaging and charming as the so-called 'Garden' carpets. The carpet is divided into twelve large compartments by rippling water channels through which shoals of fish swim in an orderly line. At the intersections light madder islands appear with blue crenellated edges; on these are woven neatly drawn blossoming trees. The carpet is also subdivided into smaller square gardens, in which are woven plane trees with multicoloured leaves or flowerbeds planted as eight-pointed stars. Dark green strips of vegetation appear at the water's edge completing the effect of a sumptuous Persian garden. The concept is thought to derive from the four-fold layout of gardens such as that of Shah Abbas's behind the Ali Qapu at Esfahan.

2 Bakhtiari garden tile rug, Chahar Mahall (detail)

dated 1906
The format and style of this more rigid pattern is clearly descended from that in *Plate 1*. The water channels, however, have been omitted, thin yellow lines appearing in their place. Series of trees, including willows, flame-shaped palmettes and vase-filled niches appear within the compartments.

3 Yomut ensi, Turkmenistan (detail)

19th century
Turkmen tribes formerly used 'door' rugs to hang over the entrance to their *yurts*. Their compartment layout suggests a wooden panelled door. However, the intersecting concourses are like abstracted versions of the channels in *Plate 1*. For the *ashik* motifs in the field, see *Abstract Shapes and Symbols, Plate 24*).

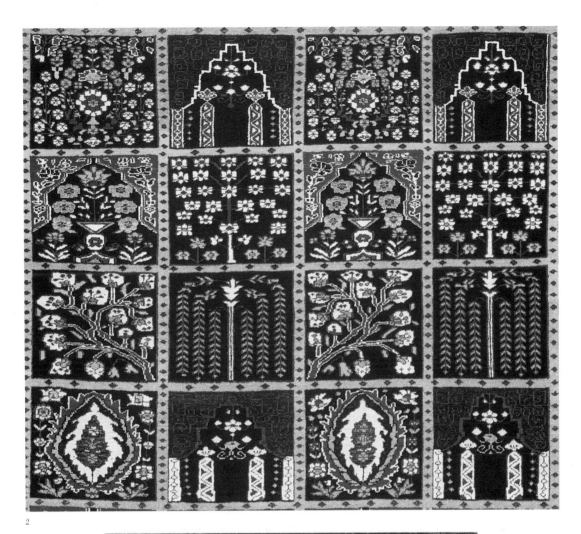

2

3

45

Compartments and Lattices

4 *South Indian sari, Karuppur, near Tanjore, Tamil Nadu (detail)*

19th century

The red-brown and white frame of these rectangular compartments is contrasted with a gold grid. Each of the rectangles contains identical simple depictions of an elephant, also in gold brocade. Such saris were made for the Rajas of Tanjore, for the royal household and for presentation to visiting dignitaries. The combination of red-brown and purple dyes with gold brocading is typical of such textiles.

5 *'Chessboard' rug, East Mediterranean region (detail)*

16th century

There is some debate as to the origin of these rugs, but their green and red palette and the execution of some of their motifs is reminiscent of the 'Mamluk' rugs of Cairo (see *Medallions, Plate 14*). This rug has a rose red ground with a repeating 'tile' design: square compartments have triangles at their four corners, thereby creating octagons. Each octagon contains a star interlace in green or turquoise around which are woven radial cypress trees. The design seems to have influenced the border found on later Anatolian rugs such as that in *Border and Guard Patterns, Plate 14*.

6 *Salor* torba, *Turkmenistan (detail)*

19th century

This design is known as *ayna khamtos* ('ayna' is the Turkish for mirror, 'khamtos', Turkmenian for 'stepped'). It comprises rectangular compartments in repeat (here two rows of seven), each filled with a single stepped diamond – outlined alter-

nately in blue and fuschia or just white. These compartments serve the purpose of primary ornaments, and like *güls* are divided into quarters of fuschia or blue-green. Simple flowerheads appear at each diamond's centre and within the quarters of the compartments.

7 *Luri kilim, Fars Region, Southwest Persia*

19th century

Intersecting dark blue lines are embellished by simple stepped devices; the resultant compartments are filled with light blue, red, yellow, emerald or white. Blocks of colour are thus contrasted in rows but form ordered diagonals. The field is further broken by the inspired asymmetry of the one red and two yellow horizontal lines of the lattice. Note also the reciprocal stepped trefoil border which is so typical of flatweaves from Southern Persia (see *Border and Guard Patterns, Plate 18*).

8 *Kurdish (?) rug, Azerbaijan (?)*

19th century

A meandering pink tendril emphasizes the division of this rug into eight square compartments. Each of these is filled with either stylised trees with 'C' shaped branches or stepped chevrons in bright colours. Mostly the heavily abrashed blue ground penetrates the compartments, but three by contrast are red. Note also the border, which is a simplification of the kufesque border (see *Border and Guard Patterns, Plates 1-3*).

4

5

6

7

8

Compartments and Lattices

9 Northwest Persian carpet
17th century
Two ogival lattice systems, one in pink, the other yellow, are set against a lustrous green – an unusual ground colour. Angular uniform buds burst forth from the pink lattice, which encompasses several kinds of palmette and flowerhead; these in turn fall at the intersections of the second lattice of thin yellow.

10 Bergama carpet, Western Anatolia
early 18th century
Orange serrated spray forms are placed together on a deep red ground to form a cleanly drawn lattice, not dissimilar in shape to that in *Plate 11*. Without the strong colour contrast between lattice and ground, the piece would perhaps not appear so compartmentalised; rather the sprays of the trellis would merge with those of the primary ornaments within to create the impression of many interlocking hexagons.

11 Shirvan prayer rug, East Caucasus (detail)
early 19th century
This finely knotted rug has a correspondingly intricate pattern. Hexagonal compartments are formed by a lattice of flames on a blue-black ground. These are filled with many different varieties of stylised flowers, each type corresponding down to the minutest detail.

9

10

11

Compartments and Lattices

12 Chinese carpet
first half 19th century
The field design of this carpet is
sometimes referred to as the *ju'i*
medallion or as *Yün Tsai T'ou* in
Chinese. Small medallions made
up of four horn-shaped brackets
are contrasted with a blood red
ground to create a grand pattern.
The design is firmly rooted in
17th- and 18th-century Chinese
carpets, but also appears in some
weaving traditions of East
Turkestan (see, for example, the
cartouches in the border of
Flowers, Plate 8).

**13 Salor trapping, Turkmenia
(detail)**
19th century
The *aksu* (the Turkish word for
'white water' or 'stream') pattern is
composed of a lattice of rectilinear
brackets framing offset rows of
abstract ornaments with protruding pincer shapes. The lattice itself
is executed in white on a dark
emerald-blue ground.

**14 Kashan carpet, Central
Persia**
late 19th century
This urban-produced carpet is
remarkable for the clarity of its
drawing. Quatrefoils and stars are
placed together in a tessellation.
Within the resultant compartments appear an array of different
vase, palmette and tree shapes.
The pattern is known as the
Joshaquani design after a town due
south of Kashan, where carpets
with such formats were made in
abundance. The 'tiles' are so closely compacted that they create the
impression of a carpet with no
single ground colour.

12

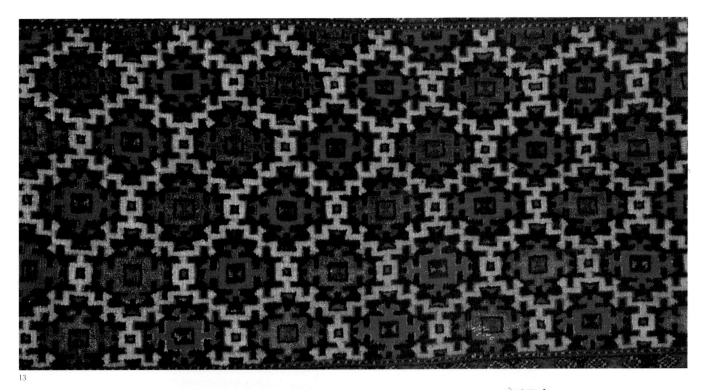

13

14

Compartments and Lattices

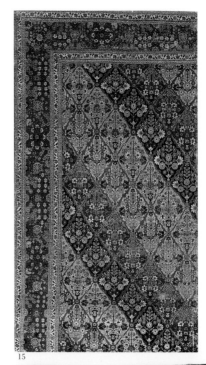

15

15 Kashmir carpet, India
18th century
Floral elements and neatly woven palmettes very close in design to many of those which appear in *Flowers, Plate 10*, are set within a naturalistic foliate lattice. Note also the close resemblance of the border to that of *Flowers, Plate 9*, another Indian example: on both a burgundy border is framed by a brilliant white guard within two 'S' guards. The realistic foliate lattice was not new to Indian weavers in the 18th century; indeed, the carpet in *Flowers, Plate 2*, which may be dated to the early 17th century, uses a more finely knotted and intricate version of a similar lattice.

16 Dragon carpet, The Caucasus
17th century
Diagonal saw-shaped leaves in white and green intersect to form lozenge-shaped compartments on a red ground (the usual ground colour for carpets of this group). Thus, a two-layer lattice is suggested, with a green lattice overlying a white one. Within the smaller lozenges are woven stylised palmettes, some shaped like pinecones. Further palmettes and layered flowerheads in beige and light blue appear at the intersections. The noble and highly prized 'Dragon carpets' take their name from the stylised 'S' shaped creatures which here appear in the uppermost lozenges and in the second row from the bottom. The motifs and format of these carpets appear to have antecedents in the weaving tradition of Safavid Persia (for which see *Medallions, Plate 2*). The strong design and colour on these carpets influenced a number of near Eastern weaving traditions, most especially Caucasian traditions of the 19th century.

17 The Scarisbrick carpet, England (detail)
c.1860
A gold and brown lattice, broken by two large star-medallions, cuts through a rich red ground. At the intersections, small medallions are variously filled with birds or the letters 'A' and 'S'. The initials stand for Anne Scarisbrick for whom the carpet was designed by Edward Pugin, son of A. W. N. Pugin (1812-52). Several 19th-century architects took an interest in textile design, the Pugins among them. The simple floral forms of the field on this carpet perhaps conform to the elder Pugin's exhortation that artists 'disposed the leaves and flowers of which their design was composed into geometrical forms and figures' (from *Floriated Ornament*, 1849).

18 'Noh' robe, Japan
18th century, Edo period
This orange and gold brocade 'Karaginu' was used for the male principal role in Noh plays, which derived from certain Japanese religious dances, and are still performed today. Rhomboid devices appear at and between the intersections of this lattice. Two types of rosette, arranged in columns, fall within the resultant compartments, one disc shaped, the other lobed.

16

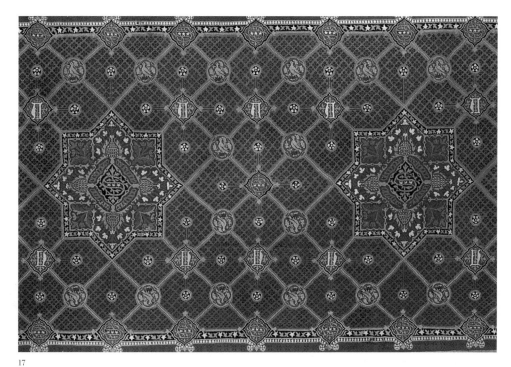

17

18

Medallions

Much is made of the similarities of the medallion and corner (or spandrel) format on Near Eastern carpets to the designs of 16th- and 17th-century embossed leather book covers and to the layouts of domed architectural interiors. From the assumption that at this time the same court ateliers that designed carpets were responsible for interior decoration and the arts of the book, it is inferred that patterns for weaving owed much to these other media. Certainly, Ottoman *yastiks* like that in *Plate 15* can be very reminiscent of book covers. However, medallion and corner carpets abound outside court weaving traditions and also appear on earlier Anatolian village rugs which could themselveshave influenced later Persian design.

This chapter contains five 'classical' weavings from Safavid Persia (*Plates 1, 2, 3 6* and *7*), a period in which large central medallions were almost *de rigueur*. Certain features of medallions from this tradition also appear on contemporaneous pieces from Anatolia, despite the fact that Safavid Persia and the Ottoman Empire were at war for much of this period. So, the arabesques within the medallion in *Plate 2* can also be found within *Plate 11*. The medallions in *Plates 1* and *8* are both lobed (although the latter is rounder) and are delineated with an intricately drawn yellow outline.

In *Plate 7* a larger medallion suggested by two niches at either end of the rug contains a smaller medallion (here a quatrefoil); this device is also found on *Plates 10* and *12*. The combination of a medallion running the length of the field with a smaller medallion at its centre is also found on *Plates 9* and *15*, and was adopted in 19th-century Persian traditions (*Plates 4* and *7*).

Medallions can be used in a number of formats, not simply in conjunction with spandrels. Sometimes a medallion (with pendants) can be used alone on a plain field to great effect (*Plates 13* and *26*). Another variation is the 'two-one-two' format, where individual ornaments entirely different from the main medallion are introduced (*Plates 21* and *22*) into the field instead of spandrels.

In general, medallions are defined purely by their function within a format; they are large central ornaments superimposed on a field. However, sometimes the term may be used to refer to a variety of medallion-like shapes repeated throughout a field (*Plates 3* and *16*), a format rigorously adhered to by many Turkmen tribes (see *Octagons and Güls*). In *Plate 3*, for example, ogival medallions (like the ogival medallion in *Plate 6*) are repeated throughout the field with cartouche pendants.

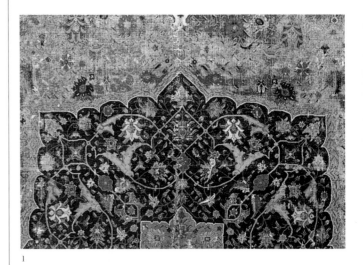

1

1 *Tabriz (?) medallion carpet, Northwest Persia (detail)*
early 16th century
This graceful rich green lobed medallion outlined by yellow leaf forms fills almost the entire width of the field. Like that in *Plate 2* it is decorated with large arabesques and scrolling vines; an eight-pointed star is woven at its centre. This pattern was to influence some later carpets from Anatolia (see *Plate 8*).

2 *The 'Ardabil' carpet, Northwest Persia*
dated 946 AH (AD 1539-40)
Arguably the most famous oriental carpet in the world, and an undoubted technical and aesthetic triumph, the 'Ardabil' carpet is a good example of the medallion-and-corner design. It is named after a town in northernmost Persia, from whose shrine the carpet was supposedly purchased and for which the carpet was perhaps woven. Here, Shah Ismail and Sheikh Sefi-ud-Din, his ancestor, after whom the Safavid dynasty (see *Palmettes, Plate 2*) was named are buried. The medallion-and-corner (these corners are sometimes referred to as spandrels) format of the Ardabil is symmetrical along the vertical axis. Each of the corners corresponds to one quarter of the central medallion. The medallion itself has sixteen points and a yellow ground with an octofoil at its centre which is echoed in the border ornaments (this border was to have considerable influence on Mughal carpets like *Border and Guard Patterns, Plate 11*). At each of the medallion's points appear ogival appendages, a feature which was to be copied by a number of early 20th-century Persian carpet designers. From both the upper- and lowermost ogive hangs a lamp, which recalls the pendants that sometimes hang from niches in prayer rugs (see, for example, *Niches, Plate 2*).

Medallions

3 *Kirman carpet, South Persia*
c.1600
Pictorial ogival medallions are
alternated throughout the field
with bird-filled or floral cartouches. Both medallions and cartouches are close in design to those in
Plate 6. The carpet may be interpreted as having eight octagonal
compartments with rich red
grounds in two columns. Mythical
creatures interlace in the border to
create lobed roundels of great
artistic merit.

**4 *Mohtashem Kashan carpet,
Central Persia***
c.1900
At first glance, this carpet has a
simple elongated medallion in red-
brown which owes much to its
'Polonaise' predecessor (*Plate 7*).
However, a medallion-and-corner
format is suggested in dark blue.
The pattern is successful for its
remarkable symmetry and precision. Note the *bid majnun* motifs
used at selected points in the field
(see *Trees and Leaves, Plate 31*).

**5 *Heriz carpet, Northwest
Persia***
19th century
This carpet shares many features
with its Persian relatives, but ren-
ders them in a rectilinear manner
typical of carpets produced on
looms in Persian villages (as
opposed to those produced to
more precise specifications in
urban workshops). Interestingly,
the corners of the field have been
resolved with pendant-like shapes
sculpted in a luscious green and
echoed in light blue within the
large medallion. Note also the

samovar border (see *Border and
Guard Patterns, Plate 13*).

**6 *The 'Padishah' silk kilim,
Esfahan, Central Persia***
late 16th century
It is interesting to note the effect
that a difference in technique can
have on a weaving's overall
impact. A simplified design sets
this flatweave apart from its pilewoven counterparts. At each end
of a light green ogival medallion is
woven a single cartouche and a
trefoil pendant. As with the almost
contemporary Ardabil carpet
(*Plate 2*), the format is symmetrical
along the vertical axis (and also
along the horizontal one); however, here the spandrels do not
represent quarters of the medallion itself and are also a different
colour. A dragon and phoenix in
conflict, a popular theme in oriental art (see *Figura-tive Motifs and
Patterns, 28*) grace the central
medallion.

**7 *'Polonaise' carpet, Esfahan,
Central Persia (detail)***
early 17th century
The format of this rug is very subtle; at one level the central medallion is simply the beige floriate
quatrefoil with a golden brown
octofoil at its centre and palmettes
within each petal. The spandrels in
the corners reflect this ornament.
However, a thin dark blue line
which runs through green octofoils
at the rug's borders creates an
elongated medallion which runs
the length of the field.

3

4

5

6

7

Medallions

8 East Anatolian carpet (detail)

late 16th century

This cloud-like medallion seems to derive its form from certain Safavid carpets – particularly a group thought to have been woven in Tabriz, Persia's capital at the beginning of the 16th century (*Plate 1*) – but has been rendered more naively. The Turks were at war with Persia during this period, but some cultural exchange seems to have taken place, as this carpet demonstrates.

9 Central Anatolian rug (detail)

first half 19th century

A small rosette-filled, light blue hexagon forms the centre of a hooked cruciform medallion made up of four white polygons outlined in a sumptuous red-orange. Two simplified cartouche shapes grow out of the larger blue-ground hexag-onal stepped medallion, but rather than leaving a plain red-orange field, the weaver introduced blue corners into which arrow shapes from the resulting large medallion protrude. This rug resolutely shuns the refinement of its classical precursors.

10 'Transylvanian' rug, West Anatolia (detail)

17th century

The name 'Transylvanian' has become attached to a characteristic type of small rug with a medallion design which appears to derive from the double-niche formats of so-called 'Small Medallion Ushaks' (see *Plate 12*). Such rugs were found in large quantities in the Protestant churches of former Transylvania, as well as in

Hungarian collections. Indeed, Hungary appears to have been a major market for Turkish rugs in the 17th century. (For the samovar filled cartouche, see *Border and Guard Patterns, Plate 10*).

11 Large Medallion Ushak, West Anatolia (detail)

c.1500

Such carpets are the cultural cousins of the Safavid carpets of Persia, and although not as finely executed, they retain a singular courtly Ottoman identity. The arabesques, pendants and other motifs all appear on Safavid carpets, but here they are more stylised and angular. As in *Plate 1*, the medallion is crenellated, but unlike its Persian counterparts, this piece uses half of a star-medallion in green instead of a spandrel.

12 Small Medallion Ushak, West Anatolia (detail)

mid 16th century

Two sculpted niches – one with a pendant – point towards the border, creating four spandrels and suggesting a large medallion. However, the rug's focal point is clearly its beautifully drawn, scalloped hexagonal medallion. The azure blue ornament within corresponds closely to the yellow arabesques within the larger medallion of *Plate 11*, its cousin. The format of this rug was to prove highly influential on later Turkish rugs, most notably so-called 'Transylvanians' which typically also have a medallion within a double-niche (*Plate 10*).

8

9

10

11

12

Medallions

13 *The New York Medallion and Pendant rug, Northwest Persia or surrounding regions*

18th century

This magnificent rug has all the grandeur of the classical Persian medallion pieces, to which it owes much, but achieves a certain informality through its plain zigzag field (see also *Palmettes, Plate 16*) and the more primal designs within the medallion. The medallion and its pendants are so distinctly drawn that they seem to hover above the field.

14 *Mamluk rug, Cairo, Egypt (detail)*

c.1500

A sixteen-pointed red and blue star is woven within a lobed eight-pointed star-medallion which strikingly combines yellow and green to make it the rug's focal point. Further stars within boxes make up the corner resolutions within the square centre panel, which is symmetrical along every axis. Mamluk carpets are named after the dynasty which ruled Egypt and Syria from 1250 to 1516 and have an archaicism in their design befitting objects half a millennium old.

15 *Ottoman velvet* yastik, *Turkey (detail)*

17th century

This fat circular medallion with small palmettes for pendants has proportions not unlike the medallions of the New York rug (*Plate 13*) and the Large Medallion Ushak (*Plate 11*). Tulip-decorated spandrels have been introduced which create a further madder medallion.

16 *'Small Pattern Holbein', West Anatolia (detail)*

15th century

'Small Pattern Holbein' carpets take their name from Hans Holbein the Younger (1497-1543) in whose paintings carpets with this pattern are wrongly thought to appear in abundance. The same West Anatolian weaving tradition is thought to have produced such designs as appear in *Plate 11* and on 'Lotto' carpets (*Abstract Shapes and Symbols, Plates 38 and 39*). The pattern has two main motifs: one, an octagonal 'endless knot' medallion (see also the secondary medallions in *Plate 22*), at the centre of which are stars, sometimes woven with elaborate interlace; secondly, ogival shapes grow out of quatrefoils filled with complex intertwining crosses.

13

14

15

16

Medallions

17 *Suzani, Bukhara region*
18th century
The medallion-and-corner format inspired a number of textile patterns, evidence of its enduring qualities. Suzanis tend to have all-over designs, but this example uses an oversize rosette as a medallion. Triangular corners are marked off by blue and orange tendrils.

18 *Kaitag embroidered panel, Daghestan, Northeast Caucasus*
18th century
So-called Kaitag embroideries have only come to light in the West since the dissolution of the Soviet Union. They display a wide reper-toire of patterns which rely heavily for inspiration on the designs of earlier, nearby traditions. An out-sized (when compared with the spandrels) medallion, perhaps depicting the sun, has been embroidered over a blue and white ground, which evokes crashing waves.

19 *Ningxia carpet, Western China (detail)*
18th century
The medallion and 'corners' of this elegant and restrained carpet appear on a natural ground devoid of further ornamentation. The central disc of the medallion is made up of tiles pieced together to create a jigsaw effect more com-mon on the borders of carpets from this area (see *Border and Guard Patterns, Plate 16*).

20 *Kashmir 'Moon' shawl, Northwest India*
early 19th century
Kashmir shawls use motifs and patterns which are common throughout Asian carpets and textiles, but which are technically reproduced in a way that is almost painterly. This later example has a lobed circular medallion filled with sprays and multicoloured flowerheads. The spandrels are exactly proportional quarter circles. Interestingly, the striped field has been allowed to permeate the medallion-and-corner format. (For another medallion and corner Kashmir shawl, see *Flowers, Plate 7*).

17

18

19

20

Medallions

21 'Karachop' Kazak rug, Southwest Caucasus

19th century

Kazak rugs thought to have been woven in the town of Karachop use the same format as 'Large Pattern Holbein' carpets (see *Plate 22*) of which they are clearly stylistic heirs. However, they have an entirely different aura from their predecessors through the combination of bright colours (notably, yellows, reds and greens) and a bold minimal working of the design. Star-filled hooked squares, for example, are used instead of spandrels.

22 'Large Pattern Holbein', Central Anatolia

16th century

'Large Pattern Holbein' carpets use a two-one-two format also employed on Caucasian weavings like that in *Plate 21*. A square central medallion contains a star-filled octagon very like that appearing at the centre of the stars of *Stars, Plate 5* and is encompassed by two pairs of corner 'infinite knot' medallions, like those repeated in *Plate 16*.

23 Lori-Pambak Kazak rug, Southwest Caucasus

19th century

Like many rugs woven in this part of the Caucasus, a traditional format is taken and distorted almost beyond recognition. A hooked hexagonal medallion encompasses an angular green cross. Layers of hooked polygons are attached to the medallion like stylised lamps. This border seems to be an interpretation of that in *Border and Guard Patterns, Plate 15*.

21

22

Medallions

24 Southwest (?) Persian rug

19th century

Out of an azure blue stepped medallion grow two green medallions quite like oversized cartouches, while abstract shapes and an abundance of stylised carnations decorate the field. All three medallions are filled with dots and zoomorphic motifs, and have at their centre rosettes exactly like those which appear on the long rugs of Talish in the southern Caucasus (see *Border and Guard Patterns, Plate 5*).

25 Regency Savonnerie carpet, France (detail)

first quarter 18th century

On French Aubusson and Savonnerie carpets – and indeed throughout the West – a single medallion format was very common. The French manufactories often favoured simple circles or polygons for their medallions, eschewing the pendants and other accretions of many Asian carpets. On this example, two diamond shapes outlined in pink intertwine to form a star-medallion.

26 Quashq'ai kilim, Southwest Persia (detail)

19th century

It is unusual for a kilim to have a medallion and pendant format. As one might expect with a tribal flatweave, complexities of design are avoided. The medallion comprises a simple stepped diamond, striped in yellow, blue, red, white and green and has two similarly drawn diamond pendants.

24

25

26

Niches

 Niches or mihrabs (from the Arabic for 'praying-place') are designs used on Muslim prayer rugs. Niches on rugs should point towards Mecca, indicating to a suppliant the position he should assume. Where the niche reaches its point the head was placed, with hands on either side positioned outside the niche but within the field. Often, however, the term 'prayer rug' may be a misnomer; while the design is sacred, it is also aesthetic. Some prayer rugs may have been made as hangings to serve as icons, or even for sale to non-Muslims.

Prayer rugs by their very nature require a specific type of supplementary ornamentation and decoration. Often the field within a niche is left bare or is sparsely decorated; that in *Plate 1*, for example, achieves sufficient interest by repetition of simple mihrabs alone. The fields within both *Plates 9* and *13* are similarly bare. In *Plate 2* columns and a pendant evoking grand architectural arches suffice; this effect is repeated in *Plates 11, 12* and *14*; many further niche patterns are strongly reminiscent of the shape of a mihrab of a mosque (*Plates 1, 9* and *16*).

When the field within a niche is embellished, its patterns are often directional. 'Millefleurs' carpets (see *Flowers, Plates 9* and *10*) woven with a mihrab, as in *Plate 18*, contain flowers whose direction runs from bottom to top. Those in *Plates 12* and *15* are similarly directional. Textiles and carpets woven in other formats are not constrained in this way; the flowers and palmettes on classical Persian carpets are often multi-directional.

Nowhere has the mihrab been more successful than on Turkish weavings. Prayer designs abound on the urban or village pieces made during the 18th century in Ladik (e.g. *Plate 14*), Mudjur and Ghiordes, and earlier traditions have multiple interpretations of the format. An interesting type is the so-called 'keyhole', re-entrant or Bellini rug (*Plates 5-7*), in which the direction of the mihrab proper is emphasised by a keyhole shape impinging on the field.

Great numbers of rugs were made commercially in the villages of the Caucasus and Western Iran, and became very popular in the West. Sometimes, as in *Plates 4* or *17*, a niche would be superimposed on a traditional all-over field design. Prayer rugs were not a feature of some nomadic weaving traditions. Turkmen prayer rugs like that in *Plate 9*, for instance, tend to be rare, although the workshop rugs made for commerce in the Amu Darya valley ('Beshir' rugs) were mainly woven by Turkmen (*Plate 10*).

1

1 *Anatolian* Saf *fragment, Ushak Region (?) (detail)*
16th century
The niches on this *saf* or multiple prayer rug are rendered in the simplest possible terms; they are given strength through the contrast provided by the saturated red on black. The resultant shape brings to mind grand portals on many Islamic buildings.

2 *Ottoman prayer carpet, Cairo (detail)*
16th century
'Classical' carpets such as these, produced in court ateliers, often served as prototypes for later textile traditions. Many subsequent prayer rugs were influenced by this grand, curvilinear arch and by the use of columns and pendants; often they incorporated stylistic accretions from their own or other traditions.

3 *Topkapi prayer rug, Persia (detail)*
17th century
The stylised niche on this rug, from the Topkapi Palace in Istanbul, in no way evokes architectural design. The curvilinear niche has a bottleneck and culminates in a *fleur-de-lis* motif. The borders combine two themes: at the top, cartouches are inscribed, while skilfully wrought arabesques (see *Trees and Leaves, Plates 15-19*) embellish the lower section.

4 *Shirvan prayer rug, East Caucasus (detail)*
19th century
This gabled niche appears to have been superimposed on the field. Note how, in contrast to numerous examples in this chapter, the field patterns continues above and below the niche. Simple gable niches are common on Caucasian weaving.

2

3

4

Niches

Re-entrant rugs

5 Mamluk prayer rug, Egypt
c.1500

'Bellini' (so called after the Venetian painter Gentile Bellini, ?1429-1507, in whose paintings a number of rugs with this format appear), 're-entrant' or 'keyhole' rugs comprise a niche and a 'keyhole' shape pushing up into the field from the lower border. This rug is notable for its attractive sculpted niche and its cloudband border. The red field is left plain except for a stylised bird perched on a tree, enough interest being imparted by the carefully drawn niche.

6 The Topkapi prayer rug, West (?) Anatolia (detail)
15th or early 16th century

The decorative band which forms the niche and the more substantial 'keyhole' is separate from the innermost border, creating a floating effect. The keyhole itself is octagonal and contains 'concentric' stars and inward pointing arrows in black and white (see also the rosette found in *Border and Guard Patterns, Plate 5*). It is unusual to encounter as many as five pendants within the niche.

7 West Anatolian rug
c.1700

Here a narrower 'keyhole' than that in *Plate 5* is echoed by a 'lamp' hanging from the niche by a chain. The gable-like niche itself is composed simply of straight lines. The 'ragged palmette' border used here is common on re-entrant rugs (see *Plate 7*).

8 Double re-entrant rug, Bergama, West Anatolia
18th century

On this rug, the niche has been dispensed with altogether. It never the less demonstrates an interesting innovation with a device usually combined with a niche. Two 'keyhole' shapes protrude on the field, created by a blue strip with elongated 'S' shapes. This rug and that in *Plate 8* share what is known as the 'ragged palmette border'. The focal point of both is a star-filled layered medallion, here encompassed by four complex triangles.

5

6

7

8

Niches

9 Turkmen (?) prayer rug, Northeast Persia (?)

mid 19th century

Here the scalloped arch is supported by two *botehs* which create a bottleneck and echo the main border ornaments. This rug could be a tribal interpretation of an architectural niche on an earlier urban-produced weaving.

10 Beshir prayer rug, Turkmenistan (detail)

19th century

A red niche culminating in a pair of hooks falls within a similar, but larger, white niche. The large stylised shrubs within the former are echoed in the inverted shrubs of the latter. Beshir rugs were often woven in workshops for commerce, and it is doubtful whether such pieces were ever actually used for prayer.

11 Village prayer rug, Konya, Anatolia (detail)

18th century

This rug shares the format seen in *Plates 12* and *14*, although here the resemblance to an architectural form is more striking. Note also the zoomorphic designs within the green field. For a similar border, see *Border and Guard Patterns, Plate 4*.

12 Silk Heriz rug, Northwest Persia (detail)

19th century

This rug immaculately reproduces the two column within a niche format. The field is filled with Persianate ornaments, typical of those found in urban-produced carpets.

13 Mudjur prayer rug, Central Anatolia (detail)

c.1800

Here the niche is woven in its simplest terms with a stepped mihrab. Apart from the green hooks that break into it, the madder field is left bare to good effect. (For another stepped mihrab, see *Trees and Leaves, Plate 27*).

14 Prayer rug, Ladik, Anatolia (detail)

dated 1187 AH (AD 1773)

Ladik rugs are typically decorated with a triple arch supported by slender columns that clearly look to early court carpets such as that in *Plate 2* for their inspiration. There are additional minor niches at the base of the inverted tulips in the lower compartment of the field.

9

10

11

12

13

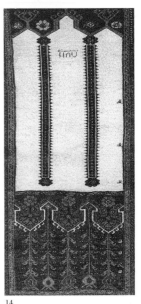

14

Niches

15 Rectangular tent side panel, Rasht (?), North Persia
early 19th century
This almost garish panel consists of a patchwork of minute pieces of broadcloth of different colours, portions of which are decorated with needlework. Here the shape of the arch is architectural. Enclosing a silver-thread urn with flowering plants and birds, it echoes the tile-work panels of early Qajar architecture (late 18th century), and the prayer-format 'millefleurs' rugs of Kashmir (see *Flowers, Plate 9*) and Persia (see *Plate 18*).

16 Anatolian kilim (detail)
18th century or earlier
These 'niches-within-niches' evoke architectural shapes, the arrowheads at their sides minarets. Each niche is mirrored down the kilim's central axis. The design brings to mind the archaic *parmakli* pattern (see *Abstract Shapes and Symbols, Plate 37*) which appears on Anatolian and Caucasian slit-weave tapestries. The finger-like finish to the niches is common on, and to some extent a result of the limitations of, flat-woven pieces.

17 Sehna prayer kilim, Sanandaj Region, Northwest Persia (detail)
second half 19th century
A sophisticated niche encloses a clearly rendered all-over *boteh* design like that of *Trees and Leaves, Plate 9*. There is a notably strong contrast between the carefully ordered *botehs* on a blue ground within the niche and the more random floral forms on white without.

18 Qashqa'i prayer rug, Southwest Persia
19th century
It is interesting to compare this 'millefleurs' rug with its Indian precursor *Flowers, Plate 9*. Its niche is composed of a scalloped arch resting on half-cypress trees; the 'mound' at the base of the field completes the picture. Certainly its design is close to that of its ancestor, but on the Indian version the flowers are more tightly packed and not as boldly coloured as those on their tribal counterpart.

15

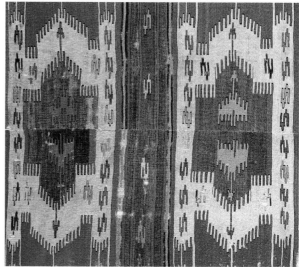

16

17

18

Figurative Motifs and Patterns

Unlike many painters, the makers of textiles tend to avoid narrative scenes or portraits, preferring abstract or stylised patterns for decoration. When figurative forms are employed (for our purposes, the floral forms represented elsewhere do not count as 'figurative'), they are often treated simply as another type of decorative motif at a weaver's disposal. Just as no animal or figure can be represented in the Qur'an, so figures are seen as anathema on many Islamic carpets. On the Sangusko carpet (*Plate 2*), the hunt scenes, angels and fauna are less prominent than the overall medallion-and-corner format of the carpet. That in *Plate 1* is the antithesis of this, and belongs to a period when Persian weavers reacted against precedent and wove rugs as portraits. Such subject-matter was inspired more by Western and Qajar paintings than by other weaving traditions.

When textiles or rugs do include figurative elements, they are often inspired by scenes from everyday life, either lofty or lowly. So, tribal weavings may depict beasts of burden, such as camels and horses (*Plates 3* and *8*). Both *Plates 12* and *13* also depict familiar scenes, although their subject-matter is more elevated. *Plate 6* contains both a hunt and a prayer ceremony, commonplace, if pivotal, acts among native American tribes.

It is not unusual for textiles to contain sacred or symbolic figurative images. So, *Plate 7*, an Indian hanging, shows cows, animals which it is forbidden to kill among Hindu cultures. The lions in *Plate 4* and the dragons in *Plates 24* and *26* are woven among so many symbols and are so evocative in themselves, that it is difficult to regard them as purely decorative. Perhaps, however, the most widespread image in all textile art cherished for its sacred potency is the bird. This is well demonstrated by the Peruvian shroud fragment (*Plate 15*), though many Near and Central Asian weavings contain birds which are thought to be similarly significant (*Plates 14* and *16*; see also *Abstract Shapes and Symbols, Plate 32*). By contrast, the bird in *Plate 17* signifies civic status. Often textiles are more overtly religious and contain actual deities. This is most clearly seen in Buddhist traditions in the Far East and on the Indian subcontinent. Although stylistically very different, the examples in *Plates 9* and *11* both show the god Vishnu, while that in *Plate 10* actually depicts a Buddha. Many pre-Columbian textiles from Peru contain stylised interpretations of deities (*Plates 21-23*). Nevertheless, figurative elements are often used simply for their aesthetic qualities. Both *Plates 19* and *20* show birds which, although derived from symbolic images, are cherished for their attractive shapes; in both examples, plumage has been used to maximum decorative effect.

1

1 *Jozan rug, Arak Region, West Persia (detail)*
late 19th century
Details of the hair, crown, pose and the monumental effect of the imposing central figure closely resemble those on the large statue of the Sasanid King Shapur I (r. AD 241-72), discovered in a cave near Kazerun in Fars Province, southwest Persia. Weavers in 19th-century Persia dramatically reacted against Islamic prohibitions to depict the large-scale human form on rugs. Such weavings were in part inspired by Western portrait painting and the advent of photography.

2 *The Sangusko carpet, Kirman, South Persia*
late 16th or early 17th century
'In perfection of detail the better carpets of this group yield to none....The animals equal those on any other Persian carpets. The *fêng-huang* is all but indispensable, appearing wherever there are animal motifs, and the best of them are rendered with a free vigour and bold sweep that even the Chinese originators did not surpass. The dragons on the Sangusko carpet are by all odds the finest to be found in Persian carpet design....The naturalistic animals are equally vital and convincing'. (Arthur Upman Pope, *A Survey of Persian Art*, 1939, pp. 2347-58). Intertwined dragons in combat (see also those in the border of *Medallions, Plate 3*) appear at the centre of the strapwork medallion. In the border ogives are filled with angel figures (echoing the ogives in the medallion), octofoils with deer and wildcats fighting, while in the spandrels, the hunt is in active progress.

2

Figurative Motifs and Patterns

3 *Yomut* asmalyk, *Turkmenistan*
19th century
The upper border of this tribal weaving depicts people, horses and dromedaries in a wedding caravan. The figures of this tribal piece lack the attention to detail of workshop weavings (e.g. *Plate 2*). *Asmalyks* are made to decorate camels for Yomut wedding processions and have even been woven on the sides of the camels.

4 *Chinese carpet*
c.1600
This carpet takes its theme – lions playing with a ball – from Buddhist iconography. The ball is most likely the flaming pearl, as seen in *Plates 24* and *26*. The field is filled with cloudbands (see *Abstract Shapes and Symbols, Plates 1-6*) and other symbols including a rhinoceros horn cup, a conch shell and a book. The 'T' inner guard, the palmette and vine border and the swastika outer guard are all typical of early Chinese rugs (see *Border and Guard Patterns, Plate 16*).

5 *Mughal carpet fragment, Fatehpur-Sikri or Lahore (detail)*
c.1600
This is one of a highly collectable group of red-ground carpet fragments, filled with images of animals and monsters. The immediate antecedents of the design probably lie in the widespread use of grotesque imagery in both Eastern and Western art in the 15th century and earlier: in Eastern sources it can be traced to the third millennium BC. The centrepiece of this fragment is a pox-ridden lion's head attached to further animal grotesques by snakes. Meanwhile, many different beasts devour each other in a carnivorous orgy.

6 *American Plains Indian painted hide, Shoshoni Tribe*
19th century
This painted hide depicts the prayer ceremony for the return of the buffalo from winter migration, using a variety of rich colours against a yellow smoke-tanned ground. Head-dressed men dance around a 'sun-dance' pole near a geometrically depicted tepee. Hunted buffaloes flee towards the edge of the hide. Though not strictly a textile, it provides an interesting contrast with Persianate versions of a hunting theme (see the spandrels in *Plate 2*).

7 *Embroidered* pichavai (hanging), India (detail)
18th or 19th century
Naturalistically embroidered cows with bells around their necks are repeated through the field. The textile has been woven in two pieces, cows on one side facing the cows on the other, kissing at the centre, where the two halves have been sewn together.

8 Sileh, *the Caucasus (detail)*
last quarter 19th century
This central panel from a flatwoven cover has been embroidered with horses and riders, birds, and a dromedary as well as a Bactrian camel. In the field two-headed quadrupeds resembling the secondary figures in *Plate 16*, for example, are embroidered in a repeat pattern. The *sumakh* technique limits the weaver to a rectilinear depiction where horizontal and vertical lines predominate.

3

4

5

6

7

8

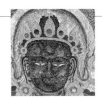

Figurative Motifs and Patterns

9 *Nepalese embroidery (detail)*
early 15th century
Combining Buddhist (see also *Plate 10*), Vaishnavite and Shaivite iconography, this pieced-together embroidery depicts a variety of divine beings in different colours. These compartments contain peaceful deities in a pose sometimes associated with 'bohisattvas', enlightened beings who have renounced Buddhahood in order to help mortals to salvation. Each carries attributes normally associated with Vishnu or Shiva – rosaries, axes, a scroll, a snake and a drum.

10 *Embroidered silk* thanka, *China (detail)*
Yongle period (1403-24)
Embroideries such as this hanging, probably commissioned by the Emperor Yongle, owe their composition to the painted *thankas* of the Tibetan tradition. Using a dazzling array of colours, it depicts Akshobhya, one of the five Dhyani Buddhas, the contours of whose body are all precisely delineated by parallel rows of satin stitch. Note especially the attention to detail on the hands and feet. The deity and the lotus pedestal on which he is seated are depicted in a similar, but more sophisticated way, to those in *Plate 9*.

11 *Silk* lampas, *Assam, Northeast India (detail)*
17th century
In 16th-century Assam, Ankaradeva, a charismatic Hindu holy man, initiated the use of figured silk cloths as altar covers. These depict scenes from the incarnations of the god Vishnu. Snakes with oversized heads and short coiled tails are repeated in strips throughout the field, while numerous avatars, or incarnations, of Vishnu, are also intricately depicted. In the trees Krishna is playing his flute, but he is so small that at first he is invisible.

12 *Silk embroidered coat, Kashan*
c.1600
Comparatively few long-stitch embroideries have survived; those that have, tend to have dark blue-black, brown or, as here, black grounds, which highlight the minimally drawn figures. Among cypress trees, birds, and beautifully curved branches, minions carrying bows or blue peacocks attend to their overlords. Of note are the omission of facial features and the florally decorated costumes of the figures.

13 Rumal *(coverlet), Golconda, Petaboli, South India (detail)*
c.1640-50
This painted and drawn textile is decorated with scenes of entertainment and merry-making, around a medallion. Two lovers embrace and several play musical instruments. One on horseback hunts a tiger. Others appear to hunt on the back of an elephant. The whole is set against a background of exotic flowers and trees. The fact that the *rumal* is painted and drawn allows for far greater delineation of the characters than on that in *Plate 12*, for example.

9

10

11

12

13

Figurative Motifs and Patterns

14 Baluch rug, Northeast Persia (detail)

19th century

Highly stylised birds, with tails fanned out in a way which brings to mind the peacock, appear in an all-over design. These charming birds have been woven in three colours, white, orange and red, which are used to create diagonal lines running through the field. A similar effect through variation of colour is seen in *Stars, Plate 7*.

15 Late Paracas or Proto-Nazca embroidered shroud fragment, South Coast, Peru (detail)

c.300-100 BC

Double-headed condors (see also the eagles in *Plate 20*) or mytho-logical birds in red, black or yellow are repeated over a rich green ground. Comb shapes in the birds' wings suggest their skeleton and, with chequers and zigzags, serve to embellish their bodies. Each con-dor holds in its talons snakes, wrig-gling to free themselves.

16 Tekke asmalyk, Turkmenistan

18th/19th century

Appropriately set within a lattice of feather shapes, each bird depiction comprises simple geometric shapes. Catapult-like 'wings' are impressionistically woven above each bird and minimally drawn double-headed quadrupeds (like those seen in *Plate 8*) additionally grace the field. The 'curled leaf' border is also found on *Trees and Leaves, Plate 4*.

14

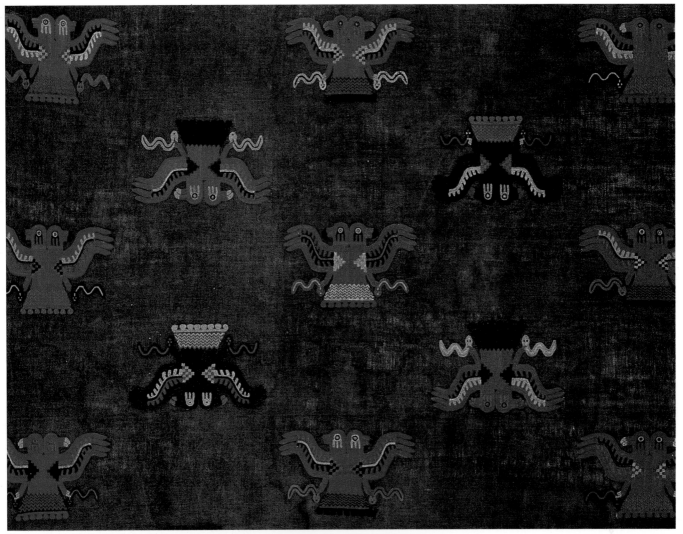

15

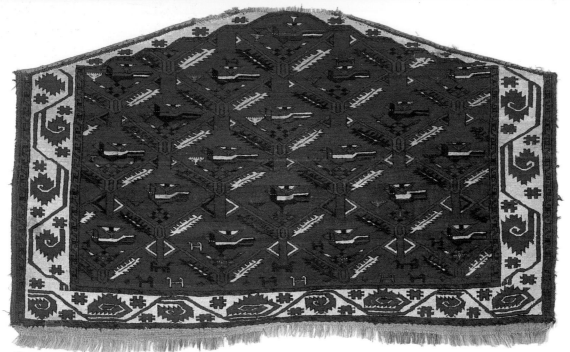

16

Figurative Motifs and Patterns

17 Silk badge of rank, China (detail)

c.1790

Symbol of the 5th rank civilian authority, this refined silver pheasant is embroidered on a dark gauze silk ground. The bird perches on one leg with outstretched wings, as if about to launch itself into the air. Cloudbands (see *Abstract Shapes and Symbols, Plates 1-6*) above the pheasant represent the air, while curved, sometimes comb-shaped waves crash beneath.

18 'Peacock and Dragon', Morris and Co., woven woollen cloth, England (detail)

designed by William Morris in 1878

The background foliage is designed in a formation of net or ogee repeats with the figures placed on top of this in pairs facing each other. Sets of peacocks and dragons repeat alternately through the width of the fabric. Of all Morris's textile designs, this is the closest he came to his early ideal of English medieval hangings. The inspiration for the design actually comes from the Middle and Far East; it has been suggested that the 'dragons' represent *fêng-huang* which had been seen by Morris on early Chinese textiles.

19 Ningxia runner, West China (detail)

18th century

At first sight the field on this magnificent piece simply comprises circular medallions alternating with elegantly drawn cloudbands (see *Abstract Shapes and Symbols, Plates 1-6*). The 'medallions' are in fact, however, cranes with wings extended over their heads. Cranes are represented in this manner commonly on Chinese carpets and textiles. The blue-beige-yellow colour scheme of this runner is typically Chinese.

20 Embroidered panel, Crete (?) (detail)

18th century

These birds have been simply embroidered on linen, with bold lines in brown, green or red suggesting their shape and form. Women fan flame-shaped dresses out at their sides and wear multicoloured crowns. More women and two-headed eagle-like birds (see also the condors in *Plate 15*) fill many of the border's lobes. Frolicking rabbits and dogs, as well as serpents wrapped around carnations, also appear.

17

18

19

20

Figurative Motifs and Patterns

21 Chimu-Inca 'Pachacamac' slit-tapestry mantle, Peru (detail)

c.1200-1400

Pre-columbian textiles are rich in anthropomorphic figures. This panel shows crescent headdress figures with arms in the air, from whom oversized duck-like birds look away. These birds are uniformly repeated throughout the field (and within the figures themselves). Each figure is differentiated by subtle colour distinctions.

22 Huari shirt or mantle, South Coast, Peru (detail)

AD c.500-1000

This textile shows four almost abstract spear-carrying deities with wings terminating in small heads. The design is strongly expressed by sections of contrasted colour.

23 Huari feather textile, Peru

AD c.500-1000

The many human figures which can be seen in featherwork such as this may represent deities. Like the creatures on the Chimu-Inca tapestry (*Plate 21*), this figure throws its hands in the air.

24 Silk imperial dragon robe, China

c.1820

A gold scaled dragon, stylistically similar to those in *Plate 26*, with a flaming body, twists around a small blue-lobed medallion; below similar creatures, clutching flaming pearls, appear in profile. The detail on this *kesi* robe, which was worn by an empress to the Emperor Tao-Kuang, is extraordinary. Small cloudbands (see *Abstract Shapes*

and Symbols, Plates 1-6) appear in profusion on a bright yellow ground.

25 Tela tirata (pulled cloth), Italy (detail)

17th century.

Angels shoot arrows at fearsome dragons to form a design unit. Note the attention paid to the dragon's wings which appear webbed. Their curved bodies combine to create a heraldic motif. *Tela tirata* refers to an unusual style of embroidery.

26 Imperial Chinese carpet (detail)

16th century

A plethora of dragons appear throughout many media in Chinese art, often woven in pairs. Flames in light brown and leaf shapes in blue, green and white appear around their twisting bodies. Note the flaming pearl between the dragons (see also *Plates 4* and *24*), a motif which dates back at least to the 11th or 12th century.

27 Dragon and phoenix rug, Anatolia (detail)

c.1400

This famous and extremely old carpet shows Chinese influences, but the theme – the dragon and phoenix in combat – is rendered in a primitive manner (see also the figures at the centre of *Plate 2*). The phoenix has jagged plumage swept over itself, while the dragon with whom it wrestles has many hooked limbs. The weaver has skilfully managed to fit these creatures within their octagonal format.

21

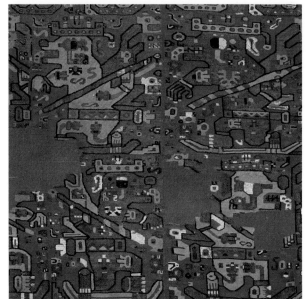

22

23

24

25

26

27

Stars

From the earliest times, stars have inspired humans and have had great religious and cultural significance. Although the examples of this chapter display important similarities, most especially in their basic shape (many woven stars are eight-pointed), they diverge in many other respects. As with so many rectilinear motifs, stars are given their most impressive treatment on Anatolian and Caucasian rugs, as is reflected by the preponderance of weavings from these areas in this chapter.

Often single stars are embellished with further, secondary stars. The 'Crivelli star' medallions (or what remains of them) in *Plate 2* have great complexity, despite being comprised of numerous simple polygons. Blocks of colour are assembled to create multiple layers of design; for example, yellow triangles are combined to create square-filled eight-pointed stars. Similarly, in *Plate 14*, inward-pointing arrowheads are juxtaposed in a circle to form a secondary sixteen-pointed star within the main ornament. *Plates 1* and *5* show a 'Russian doll' effect, with stars woven within stars. Within the star-medallions in *Plate 5*, smaller simple radial stars are combined in patterns of their own. On the Calder weaving (*Plate 10*) too we find suggestions of stars in addition to the major ornament. The colours of the simple eight-pointed stars in *Plate 7* are offset to create diagonal lines within an all-over pattern. The two-tone stars in *Plate 12*, themselves very simple, appear at once within octagons (a common combination on star patterns, see *Plate 8*) and a grid lattice.

Stars make captivating focal points as central medallions. The 'star-and-swastika' Navajo blanket (*Plate 13*) has a minimal six-pointed white star delineated with a single saw-edge black line. Central star-medallions from elsewhere include a 15th-century Mamluk carpet and a Savonnerie rooted in the Western tradition of decorative floor-covering (*Medallions, Plates 14* and *25*).

The peoples of the Caucasus show considerable ingenuity in their interpretations of simple motifs. The 'Star Kazak' (*Plate 9*) distorts its red stars by making them appear clumsy and asymmetrical; the effect is enhanced by hooks which burst forth from four points like refracted rays. The resplendent 'Lesghi star' (*Plate 1*) is complicated through the superimposed inner star with stepped shapes for points; in this way it appears almost volatile.

The star-medallions in *Plate 6* demonstrate many of the innovative characteristics peculiar to carpet production in or around Ushak in the 16th and 17th centuries (see *Medallions, Plates 11* and *12*). Instead of points, angular lobes are used, which create more space for the elaborate designs which fill the medallions. Lobes are used in the same way in *Plate 4*, enabling the weaver to introduce an array of zoomorphic shapes.

1

1 Shirvan runner, Eastern Caucasus (detail)
19th century
Few star designs can be as unabashed as the so-called 'Lesghi star', named after a region in the Caucasus where all rugs carrying this motif were originally thought to be woven, although the design seems to have been appropriated by numerous weavers of the Eastern Caucasus. Twelve-pointed stars with stepped outlines stand out from simpler twelve-pointed stars, the colours used always boldly contrasted. The overall effect is one of an explosion from the stars' centres.

2 Rug fragment, Central Anatolia (detail)
15th century
The 'Crivelli star' (named after a very similar carpet depicted in two paintings by Carlo Crivelli) is used on a variety of Turkish, Caucasian and Spanish weavings from the 15th to the 20th centuries. Here it is comprised of numerous juxtaposed geometric shapes: navy blue diamonds, bird-filled red hexagons, green hexagons with zoomorphic shapes and yellow triangles (in turn the points of a smaller star), are all combined to make a striking sixteen-pointed star.

Stars

3 West Anatolian rug (detail)
15th century
This seemingly simple rug can be interpreted in a variety of different ways. Within each large star lies a green rectangle housing a mysterious two-headed quad-ruped. Red diamonds are created where the points of adjacent stars meet. Inside these diamonds are woven star-filled octagons, repeated in sets of two at the edge of the field.

4 Sumakh *bag, South Caucasus* (detail)
19th century
This star is close in shape to the yellow-outlined star within the star-medallions of *Plate 5*. At its centre is a scalloped *gül* containing a crab-like form, to which zoomorphic shapes are appended which protrude into the star's points.

5 *Anatolian carpet (detail)*
c.1500
Ornamented or plain bands each denote a different star within this eight-pointed star-medallion; of these the 'S'-filled hexagonal cartouches of the outer strip are particularly beautiful. At the heart of these concentric stars is a 'Ninja throwing star' motif, around which green and red radial stars are woven, the former within a red octagon. The white octagon within the central medallion of *Medallions, Plate 22* is similarly embellished.

6 *Star Ushak carpet, West Anatolia (detail)*
16th century
A star-medallion is outlined in brilliant white, so that it appears to float over the red field. It comprises eight sculpted lobes around a central rectangle and is appended to a small central diamond, inlaid with stylised split flowerheads. Further medallions are suggested by stars cropped by the border, creating the impression of a field pattern which extends beyond the bounds of the carpet itself – an effect that is commonly used on rugs and textiles (see also *Octagons and Güls, Plate 7*). Further foliate elements appear within the field that typify the style of Ottoman court weavings (see also *Medallions, Plate 11*).

3

4

5

6

Stars

7 Talish rug, South Caucasus (detail)

second half 19th century

Small and very simple diamond-filled stars in yellow, blue, green and white are offset on a red field so as to create diagonal lines of a particular colour – a common effect on repeating patterns (see also *Figurative Motifs and Patterns, Plate 14* and *Abstract Shapes and Symbols, Plate 24*). The rosette-filled border is typical of that found on so-called Talish rugs; these 'rosettes' are discussed in greater detail in *Border and Guard Patterns, Plate 5*.

8 Central Anatolian rug (detail)

early 19th century

These portcullis-filled stars are created from crosses, on which stepped triangles are superimposed to form points. Octagons surround these motifs, each a medallion within four square compartments (see also *Plates 3 and 12; Octagons and Güls, Plate 17;* and *Border and Guard Patterns, Plate 2*). The design comes alive through the complicated interchange of red, light blue and aubergine within the uniform format of each compartment. Quartered stars appear in the border.

9 Kazak rug, Southeast Caucasus

early 19th century

So-called 'Star Kazak' rugs are the most prized of all post-classical (19th century or later) Caucasian village rugs, more for their bold graphic qualities than their rarity. Two different types of star, both eight-pointed make up the principal ornaments: the blue star at the centre is echoed by disproportionate half-stars cut by the top and bottom borders; two complete red star-medallions, with hooks protruding from four of their points, are more free in execution. These too are echoed by star segments in the border. The overall effect is one of an 'imprecise symmetry', with each motif enhanced by the use of a saturated palette on a white ground. Stylised green cartouches appear at diagonals around the red stars, a format which finds precedent in *Octagons and Güls, Plate 5*, also woven in the Caucasus.

7

8

9

Stars

10 'Star' by Alexander Calder
initialled and dated '75
The American artist Alexander
Calder (1898-1976) has left a great
deal of this pattern to the viewer's
imagination. This striking assy-
metrical star appears to fall within
a saw-edged circle suggested at the
left, but some of its implied points
would extend beyond the extrapo-
lated perimeter. This curving saw
edge is perhaps an incipient many-
pointed star embracing the primary motif. Linear gaps, created by
the maguey fibre tapestry technique, zigzag through the points of
the central ornament suggesting
yet more stars.

**11 Embroidered cover, Naxos
(detail)**
early 18th century
Some patterns can be interpreted
in a seemingly infinite number of
ways. Four-pointed stars in blue,
filled in with elaborately embroidered shapes, are set against propeller-like stars in red. These are
decorated with plain 'S' shapes in
white which can be read as the
constituent parts of eight-pointed
stars.

**12 Afshar (?) salt bag, Kirman
province, Persia (detail)**
19th century
Each star is brocaded in two different colours, each colour forming
propeller-like shapes reminiscent
of the four-pointed stars of *Plate
11*, or like two-tone arrow-tails. As
in *Plates 3* and *8*, and *Octagons
and Güls, Plate 17*, the stars fall
within octagons.Compartments are
created by a grid of striped lines.

**13 Navajo blanket, North
America (detail)**
19th century
This clearly drawn six-pointed
star-medallion is contrasted with a
bright red field. Its black outlines
enhance this contrast. Otherwise
the field is left bare save for four
swastika ornaments at the points of
an imaginary square – the format
is like that of two-one-two medallion carpets from Turkey and the
Caucasus (*Medallions, Plates 21
and 22*). As on *Stripes, Plate 1*, also
a product of the Navajo, the success of this pattern derives from its
stark simplicity.

**14 Pieced quilt, Northern
United States (detail)**
19th century
Light blue-grey stars within a lattice are broken down into more
complex stars by red diamonds
and arrowheads creating an eye-
dazzling effect. Small two-tone
stars are at the lattice intersections.
The quilt has been made from mis-
cellaneous pieces of cloth sewn
together.

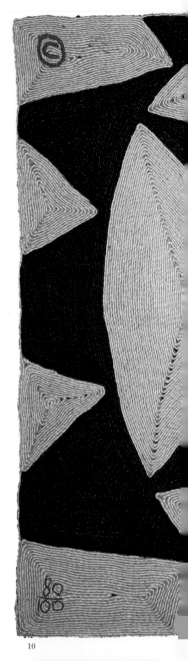

10

11

12

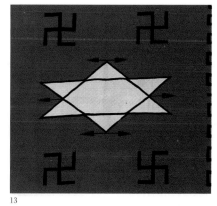

13

14

Stripes

Striped textiles are often dismissed as having designs too simple and unvaried to merit serious discussion. However, the weaving traditions which produced these textiles had numerous devices at their disposal which they would employ to make their stripes individual and characterful. Stripes are the favoured decoration of many flatweaves, partly the result of these textiles' technical characteristics – pieces so woven are better suited to simple, bold designs using large blocks of single colours than to detailed naturalism.

The stripe is used on the textiles of many disparate weaving traditions. The simplest arrangement, as exemplified by *Plates 1* and *3*, is the juxtaposition of contrasting straight-edged stripes of equal width. Almost no concession has been made to decoration or variation, although both use variegated colours. Thinner stripes appear within some of the brown-black stripes of *Plate 1* and within the raspberry stripes of *Plate 3*. The resultant 'bands' serve further to lighten the tone.

Such minimalism is generally avoided on flatweaves of the Near East. Caucasian kilims (e.g. *Plate 2*) often repeat complex arrangements of different coloured stripes to create a pattern that requires careful attention to be truly understood; it is sometimes not unlike trying to fathom a seemingly random sequence of numbers.

However, the importance of colour cannot be understated. Clearly, in *Plates 2, 7* and *8*, for example, stripes work superbly as a platform for strong contrasting colours. If these same colours had been placed together in more complex patterns, our attention would be diverted from the simple appreciation of the contrasted blocks of colour. Variety is introduced on many of these pieces through *abrash*.

Sometimes stripes are embellished with simple decorative ornaments; if stripes are of a uniform width, such additions clearly break up the pattern, and help to prevent it becoming monotonous. Diamonds break up the stripes in *Plate 5*, tiny quatrefoils the zigzags in *Plate 11*. Often a weaver uses so many decorative devices that stripes become not so much the pattern itself as the format for other patterns. So, on the South Persian kilim (*Plate 4*) a variety of patterns have been superimposed to create many 'busy' designs; the darkly coloured stripes of *Plate 6* serve to highlight the floral embroidery which appears within them.

This chapter features a number of zigzag patterns, which, like straight-edged stripes, often use interesting colour combinations for success. However, their more complex shape imparts to a textile a three-dimensional quality and gives the weaver greater scope for variation. *Plates 12, 13* and *15* adapt the regular zigzag to create original and enthralling patterns.

1

1 *Classic Navajo Chief's wearing blanket, North America (detail)*

c.1850

Between 1820 and 1880 Navajo women, living in what is now the Four Corners region of the American Southwest, wove shawl-like garments designed to be worn over the shoulders. These blankets are instantly recognisable by their stark, non-decorative striped format. Monotony is avoided through the insertion of blue-black stripes within the main bands. Strong contrasts are frequently used by the Navajo to enhance their patterns (see also *Stars, Plate 13*); here white and variegated brown-black stripes are placed together to create a captivating pattern.

2 *Kilim, East Caucasus (detail)*

mid 19th century

The primary bands – composed of thin stripes of red-brown, yellow, black and white – appear at regular intervals throughout the kilim. The stark colour combina-

tion (see also *Plate 1*), makes them the kilim's focal points. However, they are interspersed with two further types of band, used alternately: one comprising a thick red stripe bounded by two thin light-blue lines, the other, more complex, but defined by a central indigo stripe. Thin two-tone lines of brocade give further definition to some of the stripes.

3 *Aymara* iscayo *(woman's mantle), Potosi, Bolivia (detail)*

18th century

The remarkable, old textiles of the Aymara Indians are supreme in their rendering of the stripe, largely due to the great skill of the weaving. For example, subtle variegation throughout the design is brought about by spinning the wool for different yarns in different directions. The deep pink and wider purple stripes form the basic pattern. Each pink stripe is broken up by two thin blue-black lines, just as the dark bands in *Plate 1* are broken up by pairs of blue-black stripes.

2

3

Stripes

4 *Kilim, South Persia*
19th century
Tribal weavings often combine a variety of techniques to create supplementary patterns. Here, a standard striped kilim is embellished with a variety of brocaded ornaments, including flowerheads in zigzags, and with multicoloured tassels and plaited cords.

5 *Shirvan rug, East Caucasus (detail)*
19th century
The diagonal stripes of the field are contrasted with a startling red and white striped border, which brings to mind a barber's pole. Rows of rhomboid motifs appearing within the stripes break up the pattern. This charming rug combines a simplicity in conception with unabashed execution in a way that captures the best features of the weaving traditions of Caucasian villages.

6 *Zoroastrian patchwork embroided garment, Yazd, Central Persia (detail)*
19th century
The towns of Kerman and Yazd in Persia were still traditional centres of Zoroastrianism at the turn of the century, although religious persecution had forced a number of families to move to Tehran. Like other non-Muslims, Zoroastrian men were expected to adhere to dress codes out of keeping with their traditional costumes. However, Zoroastrian women seem to have been allowed more freedom, wearing embroidered garments worked on strips of different colours. The simple stripes on this example are delineated by fine lines of embroidery in black and white (see also the brocaded stripes in *Plate 2*), and are embellished with simple floral shapes.

7 *Shahsavan* jajim, *Southern Caucasus (detail)*
19th century
The pattern on this jajim appears quite simple, but the bold juxtaposition of saturated primary colours and subtle variations of width in the stripes help to make this a utilitarian object of beauty.

8 *Kilim, South Caucasus (detail)*
19th century
Striped kilims were woven in abundance throughout the Caucasus in the last century. Simple in design, their boldness is achieved through rich dark colours.

9 *Anatolian* filikli, *Karapinar (detail)*
c.1980
Simple vertical stripes in purple, yellow, blue and red are made interesting in two ways. Firstly, the long fleece-like unspun goat hair makes the pattern indistinct: strands of red appear within the blue areas and the stripes themselves are not defined by straight lines as on other textiles. Secondly the piece's texture creates an effect not unlike abrash, each stripe having darker and lighter areas.

4

5

6

7

8

9

Stripes

**10 *Flatwoven saddlebag,
Southern Caucasus***
19th century
The zigzags on this superb saddlebag are subtly stepped, a feature
which gives them a finesse atypical
of Caucasian striped flatweaves.
However, the pattern succeeds
primarily through the careful
combination of strong colours;
most appealing is the yellow used
at the bag's edges.

11 *Yomut* okbash, *Turkmenistan*
19th century
These zigzags are given character
by the great clarity with which they
have been drawn. The tiny quatrefoils which embellish them add
another dimension to the pattern
like the rhomboid motifs in *Plate
5*. The striped effect is continued
throughout what would have been
the tip of this utilitarian object.

**12 *Scane flatweave,
Scandinavia (detail)***
c.1800
Volcano-like shapes are created by
jagged zigzags uniformly drawn in
six different colours. The overall
effect is one of flawless precision
and refinement.

13 *Kilim, Azerbaijan*
mid 19th century
Jagged-edged columns, composed
of irregular diamonds placed on
top of each other, create a pattern
which has all of the starkness but
none of the symmetry of regular
zigzags. The contrast between
these columns and the red ground
on which they are woven is
enhanced by thin brown or white
outline. *Stars, Plate 13* uses similar

colour and techniques to establish
a clear distinction between ornament and field.

**14 *Southwest Persian tribal rug
(detail)***
19th century
Layers of zigzags, each outlined by
a single row of knots, impart a
three-dimensional quality to this
rug. These do not have the clarity
of the zigzags shown in *Plate 11*,
but use contrasting colours and
subtle variations of proportion to
good effect.

15 *East Anatolian rug (detail)*
18th century
This design is made complicated
by pairs of brackets attached to the
zigzags' points. These throw up
countless different shapes, and
give the impression of gables
appearing in rows throughout
the rug.

10

11

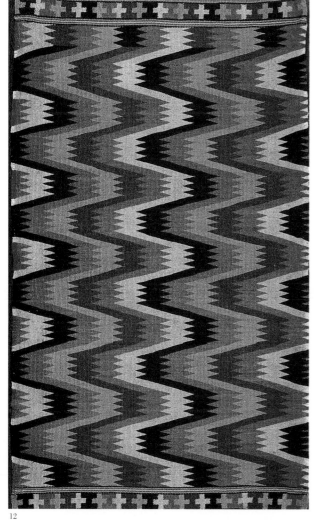

12

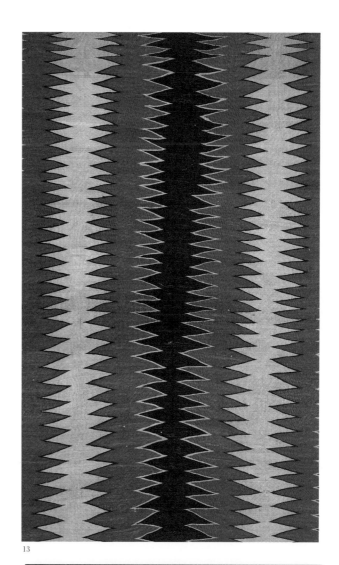

13

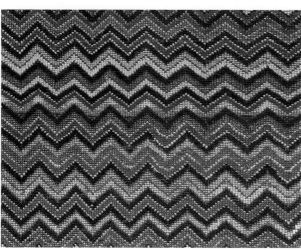

14

15

Abstract Shapes and Symbols

Many of the disparate weavings in this chapter employ abstract, and often geometric, designs, whose origins and meaning are now lost to us. Conservatism is an important feature of almost all weaving cultures: often a weaver takes over an entire design, regardless of origin or meaning. Both *Plates 35* and *36*, employ the *elibelinde* motif, thought by some to derive from primitive depictions of the Mother Goddess, whose cult is common to many Neolithic cultures. However, it seems unlikely that the motif has retained any of this original significance.

The chapter begins with six examples of the 'cloudband' – a stylised depiction of a cloud which is often symmetrical and which resembles a band knotted at its collar (other cloud motifs are often so described by extension). Whatever its origin or significance, in its many manifestations, this motif spans the whole of Asia. In *Plate 2* it is cleverly used in a re-entrant format (see *Niches, Plates 5-8*), in *Plate 3* in lieu of vases. Both *Plates 5* and *6* use idiosyncratic versions to form attractive repeat patterns.

The so-called *çintamani* design in *Plates 17, 18* and *19* is of confused ancestry – the three balls are famously represented as flaming jewels on an 11th- or 12th-century silk textile, from either China or Japan. They also appear (without the wavy lines) as a vine on a vase painting attributed to the Greek settlement at Klozomenai on the Anatolian mainland in the 6th century BC. The precise significance of the design is a matter of conjecture, but it finds its clearest expression in a variety of Turkish media.

This archaising quality of many textiles – especially flatweaves and felts – is shown by the *parmakli* design in *Plate 37*, which has been compared to a wall painting (7th millennium BC) from Çatal Hüyük in Anatolia. The Anatolian flatweaves in *Plates 10* and *31* share this archaic quality. The earliest known felts, from the 4th or 5th century BC, were found in Siberia, and the abstract design of the Kazakh felt (*Plate 12*) reflects their character and design. The brocaded flatweaves in this chapter also display a certain primitivism, inherent in the boldness and (apparent) simplicity of their designs (*Plates 8, 21* and *23*).

Few pileweaving traditions display such variety of design as those of the Caucasus (*Plates 7, 9, 30, 32* and *33*). Their conservatism is illustrated by the fact that many of their rugs can be attributed to a specific region purely on the basis of design. Quintessentially village weavings, they tend towards complex rectilinear designs which, while sometimes floriate (as in *Plates 7, 9* and *32*), are mostly abstract.

1

Cloudbands

1 The 'Chelsea' carpet, Persia (detail)
16th century
This variation on the reciprocal trefoil border (for such borders, see *Border and Guard Patterns, Plate 17*) belongs to one of the most famous carpets in the Victoria & Albert Museum, London, and provides an interesting comparison with *Plate 2*. As in the latter, a three-lobed niche, delineated in white encompasses a cloudband. This thin and graceful cloudband, drawn among arabesques and scrolling stems, is green within the carmine red niche, blue-green within the dark blue.

2 Niche rug, Anatolia (detail)
16th century
This rug intelligently uses a cloudband and a three-lobed niche in its field to create a re-entrant format (see *Niches, Plates 5-8*). Although cloudbands are common throughout Asian textile art (see *Trees and Leaves, Plate 17; Niches, Plate 5; Figurative Motifs and Patterns, Plates 4, 17, 19* and *24*), it is unusual to find a large single cloud as a rug's central motif. The cloud itself is broken up by small hooks and encompasses a colourful and crisply drawn palmette. Further asymmetrical cloudbands appear in red at the rug's centre.

2

Abstract Shapes and Symbols

3 *Northwest Persian carpet (detail)*

17th century
This beautiful carpet owes something in its design to certain vase carpets (see *Flowers, Plate 23*); here the vases, out of which grow different plants with blossom-like flowerheads, are interspersed with similarly shaped twin cloudbands.

4 *Esfahan carpet, Central Persia (detail)*

early 17th century
Large cloudbands in orange and brown are strategically placed throughout a field filled with numerous Safavid ornaments. Smaller clouds and half-clouds appear in yellow at the carpet's bottom, while (corroded) black cloudbands are woven along the central horizontal axis.

5 *Beshir carpet, Turkmenistan*

19th century
These cloudbands have none of the grandeur or intricacy of those found on 'classical' carpets (*Plates 1-4*), but are juxtaposed effectively to create a fluid abstract pattern. An interesting multi-coloured ground (including two shades of blue and a reddish brown) and a variety of smaller devices, including *botehs* (see *Trees and Leaves, Plates 9-14*) and stars enhance this effect.

6 *Ningxia rug, Western China (detail)*

18th century
Bipartite clouds, less stylised than the cloudbands in *Plates 1-5*, are repeated throughout a navy blue field. Each cloud is lobed and filled with 'C' shapes which create a feeling of three-dimensionality. The clouds are offset to create diagonal lines which suggest movement from right to left.

3

4

5

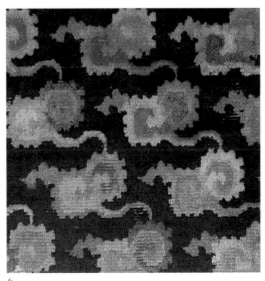

6

Abstract Shapes and Symbols

Crosses

7 Sunburst rug, Karabagh (?) region, South Caucasus (detail)
19th century
The central motif comprises a rich green cross within a white diamond, which explodes into the field. Further white crosses are suggested by white spokes which create the feeling of explosion.

8 Brocaded flatweave, Anatolia (detail)
19th century
This pattern has a complexity which yields numerous interpretations. Most striking, however, are the diamond-filled white crosses which grow out of the white vertical lines. These crosses compartmentalise the field and highlight the diamond shapes which fall between them.

9 Zeikhur rug, Northeast Caucasus (detail)
19th century
No cross motifs in the textile arts can be as heavily ornamented as those woven in the Zeikhur region. A red diamond, with complex floral palmettes at each of its four points, contains a light blue diamond-cross into which are inserted four thick, rectangular black cartouches. These connect the red diamond with green half diamonds at the edge of the field, thereby creating one cross, and suggesting four more.

10 Anatolian kilim (detail)
18th century
Subtle variations of shade give these crosses much of their

character. Their design strongly brings to mind the swastika or 'pinwheel' (see *Plates 33* and *34*). However, the crosses' success largely derives from the contrast between their strong colours and the natural ground colour. Diamond shapes – of the type which often make up the main ornament on Near Eastern kilims – embellish each cross's centre (see also the diamonds in *Plate 20*).

11 Konya runner, Central Anatolia (detail)
19th century
These crosses are deceptively simple. Four hooked gable shapes face towards a single point which becomes the intersection of the resulting diagonal cross. Each diagonal appears to culminate in hook shapes. Interestingly, the motif is reproduced within the *tauk nuska güls* of *Octagons and Güls, Plate 6*. Numerous 'five-on-a-die' crosses are randomly placed throughout the field.

12 Kazakh felt, Central Asia (detail)
c.1875
Each design unit comprises four blue inward pointing trefoil variants within an octofoil. These shapes are created by contrast with four red 'cut-outs' (not unlike curvilinear versions of the 'gables' of *Plate 11*) superimposed on the blue ground. The edges of these 'cut-outs' suggest crosses whose intersections are the focal point of each unit. The overall effect is one of dignified archaism, although the piece is little more than one hundred years old.

7

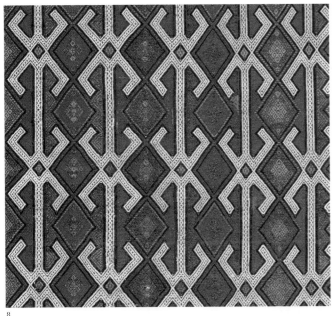

8

9

10

11

12

Abstract Shapes and Symbols

Dots and the Çintamani Design

13 Silk ikat panel, possibly Samarkand, Central Asia (detail)

19th century

Sets of six dots with 'eyes' at their centre appear throughout the field. The seemingly random use of pink, yellow, green and white for these circles creates a number of configurations: diagonals for example abound in all these colours.

14 Tie-dyed panel, Central Asia (detail)

19th century

The prevalence of 'eyes' with-in dots is perhaps partly explained by precedents set by tie-dyed textiles. Here, a multiplicity of dots are set within a carefully ordered framework. At the centre of each design unit are four green-outlined 'cherries' around a small diamond; these are encircled by red motifs outlined in white.

15 Khotan rug, East Turkestan (detail)

19th century

Once again dots are represented with 'eyes' at their centre, and are repeated throughout the field; this is known as the *P'u-lo* design. It is often associated with rugs from the northwest frontier areas of China and is supposedly derived from Tibetan 'tie-dyed' designs.

16 Tie-dyed banner, South Coast, Peru (detail)

middle/late Nazca, c. 300-700 AD

Dots punctured by small 'eyes' – a result of tie-dyeing – are repeated on a black ground so that they also appear as hoops. Blocks of red or white dots create a random striped effect. It is interesting to see disparate textile traditions achieving the same results through the same techniques (see also the minor yellow dots in *Plate 14*).

17 The Von Bode çintamani rug, Northwest Anatolia (detail)

16th century

Few designs in oriental art are as engaging as the *çintamani* (*Plates 17-19*). Typically (as here), it comprises three dots placed over a pair of wavy lines, which resemble both lips and tiger stripes. The dots appear spherical through the use of off-centre 'eyes'. These elements probably originate in painting and are repeated throughout the white field in vertical rows.

18 Village rug fragment, Central or East Anatolia (detail)

16th century

Pointed sickle shapes encompass four simple dots in a triangular configuration. Secondary ornaments of just three dots break up the pattern. The spheres have an archaic feel to them, enhanced by the peculiar antler-like shapes appearing within each sickle.

19 Kütahya tile, Anatolia

16th century

The blue and white dots suggest the eyebeads which have been used throughout much of Asia for many centuries as amulets against the 'evil eye'. Further orange 'eyes' appear within the blue. Painting is a medium well suited to the elegant curves of the *çintamani* design.

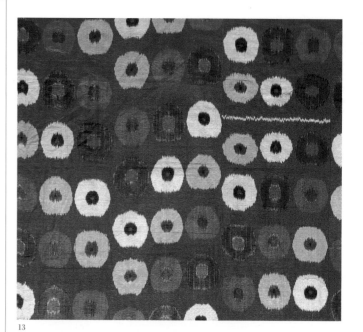

13

14

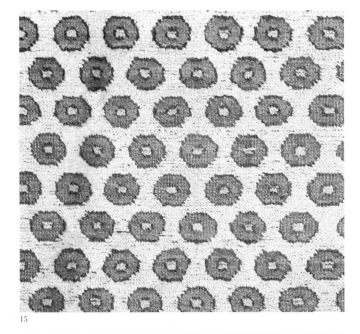

15

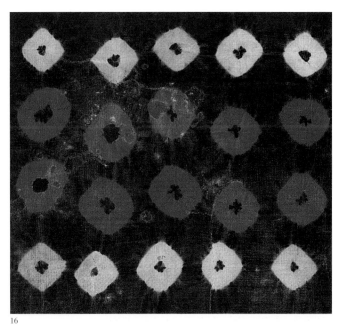

16

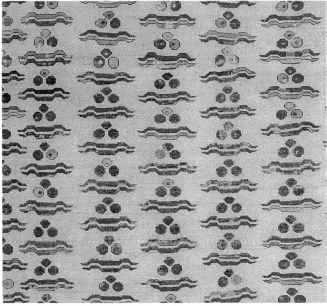

17

18

19

Abstract Shapes and Symbols

Diamonds

20 Shirvan kilim, East Caucasus (detail)

19th century
A number of ethnographic photographs show kilims of this kind draped over wagons belonging to Azerbaijani nomads. Indeed, this design and its variants are as prevalent on Caucasian kilims as stripes (see *Stripes, Plates 2 and 8*). Four hexagonal diamonds alternated with 'hourglass' triangles are woven in five rows.

21 Brocaded flatweave, Anatolia (detail)

19th century
Brocaded in white are chequered quatrefoils or crosses, with simplified shrub shapes attached to them. Within these lie diamonds, embellished with further hooked shapes like those on rugs woven by the 'Jaf' Kurds (see *Plate 26*) of Western Iran. Eight-pointed stars are suggested by the burgundy-brown field, within which appear larger diamonds, decorated with smaller stars and 'C' shapes.

22 East Anatolian rug (detail)

19th century
Just as white vertical lines join the crosses in *Plate 8*, so too here three columns of hooked diamonds are linked by narrow vertical lines; these are in turn broken up by narrow horizontal lines. In this way the rug is broken into a grid format. The diamonds themselves are filled with stars (as those in *Plate 23*) or with two pairs of triangles in hour-glass formation.

23 Brocaded flatweave, Central Anatolia (detail)

First half 19th century
Star-filled diamonds appear in diagonals across a white field. On their sides are trefoil or shrub motifs. The design is thought to derive from a 'Seljuk' pattern, which helps explain its archaic feel (the Seljuks were the ruling family of a Turkmen tribe and invaded western Asia in the 11th century, founding various dynasties in Persia, Syria and Asia Minor). The brocaded technique gives the textile a 'ribbed' appearance.

24 Chodor ensi, Turkmenistan (detail)

19th century
So-called *ashiks* are repeated throughout the cherry field in diagonals of brown and blue-black (see also *Figurative Motifs and Patterns, Plate 14; Stars, Plate 7*). These motifs are diamonds with jagged edges, here filled with simple candelabra shapes.

25 Sauj Bulaq rug, Persian Kurdistan (detail)

19th century
Saw-edged diamonds in a variety of bright and beautiful colours – apparently used at random – are set in a tessellation, in a way that is evocative of the *ashik* ornament (see *Plate 24*). The reciprocal sickle-like 'C' shapes within these diamonds can be compared with those in the aptly dubbed 'C'-*gül* (see *Octagons and Güls, Plate 19*).

20

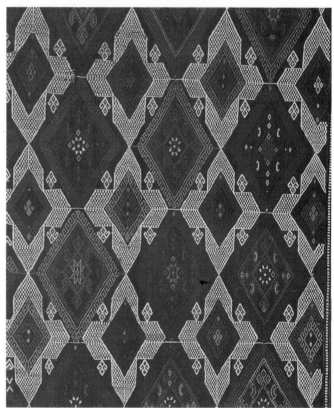

21

22

23

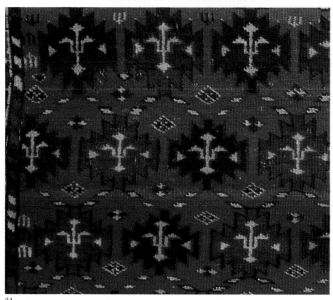

24

25

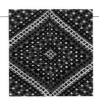

Abstract Shapes and Symbols

26

26 Jaf Kurd rug, Kermanshah Region, West Persia (detail)
19th century
This pattern typifies the weaving of the nomadic Kurdish Jaf tribe, who used to move to Mesopotamian plains during the winter months. Rows of 'concentric' hooked diamonds (compare those in *Plate 22*) are placed together in contrasting saturated colours to form a pattern open to numerous interpretations. This pattern appears on numerous saddle-bags woven by the Jaf tribe, but is rarer on rugs. Its success or failure largely depends on the combination and quality of the colours used.

27 Late classic Saltillo serape, Northern Mexico
mid 19th century
Tiny stepped diamonds are repeated in a tessellation to create an eye-dazzling effect, broken by an impressive white-outlined diamond medallion. This pattern comprises one shape – the diamond – rendered in a number of different configurations. Even the border is made up solely of diamonds.

28 Kurdish rug, Western Persia (detail)
19th century
Clearly drawn stepped diamonds appear – in three column format – on an attractive *abrashed* camel-coloured field. These diamonds are filled with smaller similar diamonds in contrasting colours, which are in turn filled with crosses.

29 West (?) Anatolian kilim (detail)
before 1800
This vibrant kilim has a pattern composed of horizontal bands on a light burgundy ground. Cartouche shapes occupy the centre of the piece like a column. These are each partly constructed from four consecutive stepped diamonds, whose presence is such that they look like the piece's major ornaments. They are woven in rich pink, red, green, aubergine and other colours; one is a brilliant white. (For the comb shapes in the field, see *Plate 37*).

Hooked Motifs

30 Lenkoran runner, South Caucasus
early 19th century
The format of this rug, which is typical of pieces woven around the town of Lenkoran, is similar to that in *Plate 31*. Three octagonal medallions are placed on top of each other. Hooked devices, filled with branch-like ornaments, surround these, producing simple crab shapes.

31 Anatolian kilim
before 1800
A vertical sequence of three hexagonal medallions from which protrude hooked devices has been woven on a light indigo ground. The resultant shapes appear zoomorphic. Each hexagon is filled with further hooked polygons not unlike the diamonds of *Plate 22*.

27

28

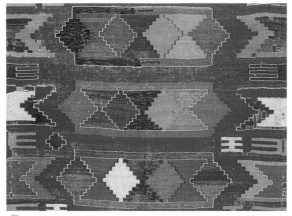

29

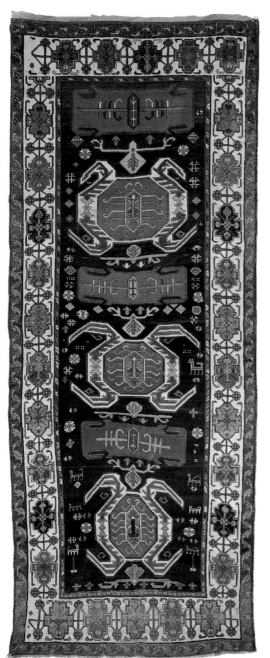

30

31

Abstract Shapes and Symbols

Other Abstract Shapes

32 'Perepedil' prayer rug, Kuba Region, East Caucasus (detail)
19th century
Around a single octagonal medallion, wild, almost zoomorphic, shapes are symmetrically placed. Two sets of four bird-like motifs occupy the points of two imaginary, concentric squares around this medallion, while the elaborate hooked motifs could be described as winged. An alternative interpretation is that these abstract shapes are derived from floral ornaments; indeed, on early 19th-century long carpets from Northwest Persia, similar hooked motifs are like abstract renditions of petals.

33 Kazak rug, Southwest Caucasus (detail)
19th century
So-called 'Pinwheel' or 'Swastika' Kazaks are highly cherished for their bold patterns, rather than for their rarity. Dark blue squares with hooks at each side are the main ornaments on this red ground rug (blue on red is the only known colour combination of this pattern on pilewoven pieces). They suggest a feeling of spinning like Catherine Wheels. Rosettes, or inward pointing arrows, similar to those on the borders of Talish rugs (see *Border and Guard Patterns, Plate 5*) are woven within each pinwheel, and as secondary ornaments on the field itself.

34 Anatolian kilim (detail)
19th century
It is very unusual to find flatwoven pinwheels. This example nicely

demonstrates the extent to which a slit-tapestry technique can affect a weaver's interpretation of a single motif. These pinwheels consist of hooked diagonal crosses and form a column down the centre of the kilim. Further pinwheels in brown and in blue (again) are suggested to either side. However, the design can be more easily read as a row of white diamond shaped medallions or cartouches (each filled with a single pinwheel), with hooked pendants attached to the piece's edges.

35 Anatolian kilim (detail)
before 1800
Elaborate blue abstract shapes are repeated in a tessellation on a natural ground. These comprise the so-called *elibelinde* motif, repeated in mirror image along the horizontal axis. The design itself is old, certainly predating this kilim, but its appearance is modern, and perhaps brings to mind the blue-on-white figures of Henri Matisse.

36 South (?) Caucasian rug (detail)
dated 1288 AH (AD 1871)
Here the *elibelinde* motif, more commonly found on Anatolian kilims such as that in *Plate 35*, is interpreted in pile; it is repeated throughout the field in three diagonal bands of different colours. Each motif has a good deal less symmetry and precision than its flatwoven counterpart, but this does not undermine the power of the design. The colour contrast between the motifs and the *abrash*ed blue ground is particularly attractive.

32

33

34

35

36

Abstract Shapes and Symbols

37 *Anatolian kilim (detail)*
before 1800
The so-called *parmakli* design
(from the Turkish for 'finger') is
common on Turkish and
Azerbaijani flatweaves. Indeed,
these comb shapes appear as
minor ornaments in *Plate 29*.
Here, simple sets of eight 'fingers',
woven in abrased light blue,
turquoise and green, are joined to
form two columns which meander
down the field.

38 *'Lotto' carpet, West Anatolia*
16th century
So-called 'Lotto' or 'Arabesque'
carpets (named after Lorenzo
Lotto, c.1480-1556, in whose
paintings such carpets can be
seen) are characterised by one of
the most engaging and effective of
all patterns in the textile arts.
Within the design unit, cruciform
quatrefoils (here running up the
carpet's centre) form with their
outline an octagon, while the hori-
zontals and verticals of the basic
linear cross mark off the angles of
a square. This complex design is
usually woven in yellow on a red
ground. On this example, the red
ground strongly suggests horizontal red strips which divide the
piece into bands.

39 *Ushak carpet, West Anatolia*
16th century
C. G. Ellis, a notable carpet scholar,
identified three variants of the
Lotto design, the 'Anatolian', the
'ornamented' and the 'kilim' styles.
Plate 38 shows an example of the
'Anatolian' style; this example typifies the 'ornamented'. This is
characterised by the emergence of
rows of circles as a secondary feature of the design.

**40 *Salt bag, Lors tribe,
Southwest Persia***
early 20th century
This warp-faced bag has repeated
black and white triangles, which
are made more interesting through
the alternation of colours that
appear as dots – white dots on
black triangles and vice-versa.
These triangles combine to form
further different sized triangles.

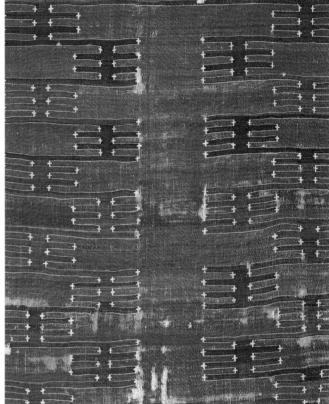

37

38

39

40

Octagons and Güls

This chapter is largely devoted to the extraordinary array of designs in the Turkmen weaver's repertoire. These distinctive Central Asian rugs, carpets and bags have remarkably similar palettes and formats. Rows of motifs (*güls*) are repeated over a madder-dyed field and alternate with cruciform devices (*Plates 6, 9, 13* and *14*) or other ornaments. These *güls* are often medallion-shaped polygons, but a number of other ornaments are used; their names are discussed in the individual captions. Often one or two compartment systems are either delineated with thin lines (*Plate 2*) in a grid or implied by the quartered design of the *güls* themselves (*Plates 6* and *9*). Each compartment can often be read as having a central medallion with spandrels at the corners made up by the secondary motifs; Small Pattern Holbein carpets like that in *Medallions, Plate 16* combine two ornaments to similar effect.

The word '*gül*' is Turkish for 'rose' and Persian for 'flower', and many of the motifs described here have floral qualities. It is interesting to note that a mid 2nd millennium BC tomb painting from Thebes in Egypt also has a pattern of medallion-like roundels repeated within dual compartments and these ornaments are very like simplified flowerheads. The lobed outlines of the '*gülli-güls*' in *Plate 1* evoke petals, while the arrow-tails in *Plate 2* are like stamens. Some *güls* contain more explicit depictions of flowers; the primary elongated *güls* and the secondary cruciform ornaments (known as *chemche güls*) in *Plate 13* both contain interpretative rosettes. Similarly, the octagons in *Plate 8* are filled with chains of daisies with hooked appendages, while the warmly coloured octagons in *Plate 11* are like sunflowers.

Two other categories of textile have been included in the chapter. Inevitably, the Turkmen repertoire of designs was taken up by a number of weaver imitators, often with good results. *Plates 9* and *14* both show adopted designs found on Turkmen rugs. By contrast, a number of less closely related repeating octagon designs have been included, demonstrating the limitations and similarities of this aesthetic. *Plates 5, 10* and *11* all show octagons combined with secondary motifs. It is perhaps sensible to think of all such designs as belonging to a much larger tradition and the result of complex cultural interaction.

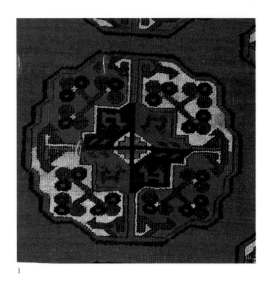

1

1 Saryk main carpet fragment, Turkmenistan (detail)
19th century
The *gülli-gül* shown here deviates from those in *Plate 3* in a few interesting particulars. The ornaments within the *gül* are divided into quarters in blue/blue-green or cherry red, creating the appearance of horizontal and vertical lines running throughout the carpet to divide it into square compartments. Also, two-headed animals (see also the *tauk nuska güls* of *Plate 6*) appear within these quarters. In pink silk, at the *gül's* centre, a segmented cross has been woven.

2 Tekke main carpet, Turkmenistan (detail)
19th century
This complex pattern is divided into square compartments, while striped lines running vertically through the secondary ornaments create further rectangular sections. The main *güls* are scalloped octagons, as in *Plates 1* and *3*, but where trefoils appear in the *gülli-güls* of those carpets, here arrow-tails penetrate the central star. It is unusual to find the 'curled leaf' (see *Trees and Leaves, Plate 4*) in the border of carpets woven by the Tekke tribe.

3 Ersari main carpet, Bukhara Emirate (detail)
19th century
The elegantly scalloped main ornament of this carpet is known as the *gülli-gül*, the standard ornament of main carpets woven by the Turkmen Ersari tribe. It is divided into quarters with a superimposed twelve-pointed star at its centre. Within each quarter appear the three sets of trefoils which are the *gül's* chief defining characteristic. Each *gül* seems to fall within an elongated octagon created by the hooked secondary ornaments.

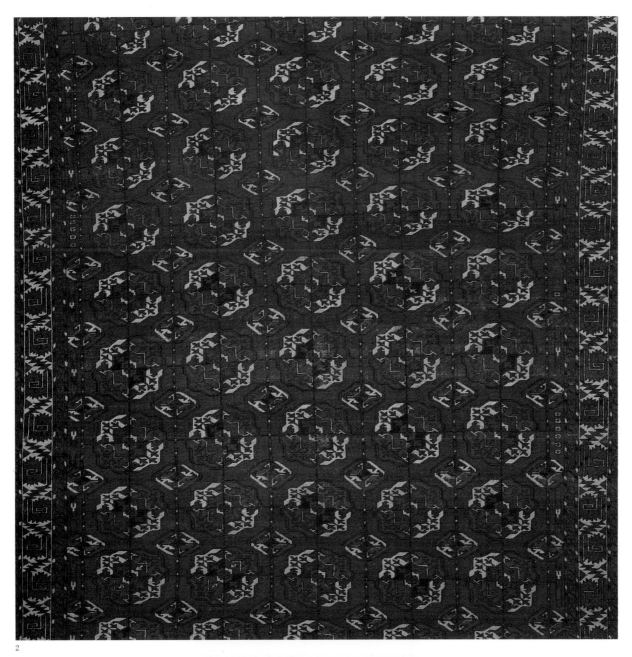

2

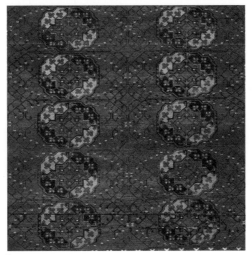

3

Octagons and Güls

4 Silk embroidery, Morocco
18th century
This octagon is filled with elaborately interlaced 'spokes' in yellow and fuschia. The effect is not unlike that of the 'endless knot' motif on early Turkish and East Mediterranean carpets, such as *Medallions, Plate 16*, which also has an octagon with a star at its centre.

5 Silk embroidery, Azerbaijan (detail)
18th century
This silk and silver thread embroidery illustrates as well as any textile the ambiguity in the interpretation of a pattern. Blue cartouches also strongly suggest a star-filled octagon in a format reminiscent of that used in *Stars, Plate 9*.

6 Yomut main carpet, Turkmenistan (detail)
19th century
The primary ornament of this carpet is the *tauk nuska gül* (see also *Plate 9*). It is characterised by the pair of two-headed creatures which fall within its quarters (as on the ornament in *Plate 1*). Cruciform devices are uniformly woven within each octagon's centre. Interestingly, these closely resemble the crosses of *Abstract Shapes and Symbols, Plate 11*. The secondary ornaments of this carpet are known as *chemche* (Turkish for 'wooden ladle' or 'spoon') *güls*, and commonly appear on Turkmen carpets and bags.

7 Salor chuval, Turkmenistan
18th century
Salor *chuvals* with the so-called Salor *gül* are highly prized by collectors of Turkmen weavings. This *gül* is octagonal and has a

jagged edge with lobed devices in black or pink. Three Salor *güls* and parts of six more intersected by the borders suggest a endless repeating pattern which transcends the confines of its borders – a common effect on all carpets and textiles. (See also *Compartments and Lattices, Plate 5*, and *Stars, Plate 6*)

8 Kansu carpet, West China (detail)
c.1800
Octagons are divided into four segments by a diagonal trellis and are linked by boxes. The 'tile' design was inspired by Ming dynasty Chinese brocades, but one can see resonances of Turkmen *güls* in these octagons. Whatever the origin of these designs, it is significant that the geometric shapes which appear on Turkmen *güls* here appear as stylised flowerheads.

9 Karakalpak rug, Central Asia (detail)
19th century
This maroon ground rug is reliant on the repertoire of the nearby Turkmen for its design. Its primary octagonal ornaments are interpretations of *tauk nuska güls*. However, only one animal has been fitted into each segment of these larger, more symmetrical octagons; unlike the Turkmen version, it has four legs and a tail appears instead of a second head. Here, at each *gül*'s centre a simple square appears, where in *Plate 6*, this is a six-pointed star. The inward pointing arrows within this square replace the cross in *Plate 6*. The secondary, diamond-shaped ornaments with appended hooks resemble *chemche güls*.

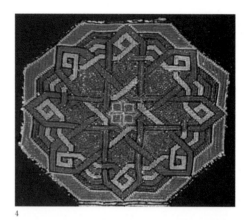

4

5

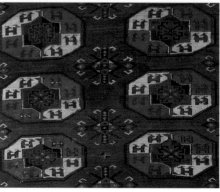

6

7

8

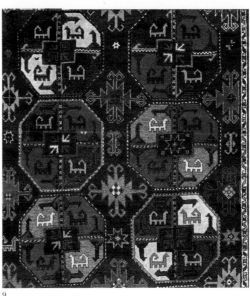

9

Octagons and Güls

10 Shirvan prayer rug, East Caucasus

19th century

This prayer rug, like that in *Plate 11*, has three juxtaposed columns of octagons. On both rugs, diamonds are used to fill the gaps between them. Again, hooks are used to fill these octagons. However, the overall effect is quite different here, perhaps as a result of the more rectilinear rendering of the rug's ornaments, and certainly due to the dramatically different palette.

11 Khotan rug, East Turkestan (detail)

early 19th century

Three columns of contiguous octagons in saturated colours are filled with hooked devices and blossoms. Together they create the impression of an abundance of sunflowers, viewed from above.

12 Yomut main carpet, West Turkmenistan (detail)

19th century

These *güls*, more minimal in character, are usually found on Turkmen *chuvals*. They are set on a deep maroon ground, with simple eight-pointed stars as secondary motifs. As in *Plate 13*, fourteen pointed stars fall within each of the main *güls*, although, quirkily, on the top row shown some of these points have been omitted.

13 Tekke torba, Turkmenistan (detail)

first half 19th century

The *chemche güls* on this beautiful six-*gül* bag divide the weaving into six rectangular compartments each filled with the primary *gül*. The latter are typically divided into four segments, and again we find a star within − although with its fourteen points it is considerably more complex than most. Both major and minor ornaments have rosettes at their centres .

14 Southeast Caucasian runner (detail)

19th century

As in *Plate 9*, we see a naive interpretation of a Turkmen ornament; these *güls* are superficially similar to those in *Plates 12* and *13*, although they have none of the finesse of these. However, the introduction of a number of different colours into the quartered framework of each *gül* helps to make this a successful pattern. Note how the compartmented structure has also been observed. Cruciform devices, like *chemche güls*, appear as secondary ornaments beside typically Caucasian motifs. Note also the 'curled leaf' border, often found on Turkmen weavings (see *Trees and Leaves, Plate 4*).

10

11

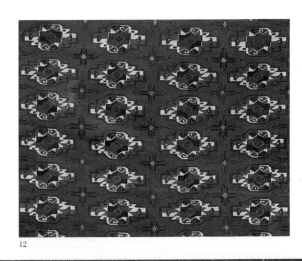

12

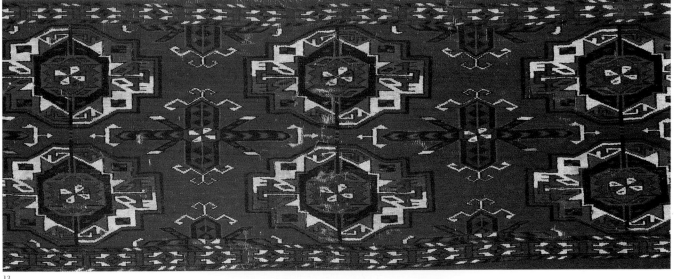

13

14

Octagons and Güls

Memling Güls

15 *Kazak rug, Southwest Caucasus*
mid 19th century
The primary ornaments on this blue ground are known as 'Memling' *güls*. This *gül* appears throughout many Asian traditions, most especially in Anatolia, the Caucasus and, indeed, on Turkmen pieces. The Thyssen-Bornemisza Collection in Lugano owns a portrait by Hans Memling (c.1430-1494) which has a floral still-life by the same master painted on the back, dated to 1480. The latter shows an Anatolian carpet, draped over a table, precisely depicted with rows of hooked stepped polygons in rows. The *güls* shown here are far less refined than the precise examples seen in *Plate 16*, although their fuller shape resembles the ornaments in the Memling painting. It is striking the difference the broader palette of this rug makes. Hooked cruciform devices in contrasting colours appear within the *güls* themselves.

16 *Yomut* torba, *Turkmenistan*
mid 19th century
The crisply drawn Memling *güls* on this magnificent bag are filled with stars, as indeed are some of the primary ornaments in the Memling painting. Here the dark blue hooks give the piece great definition.

17 Yatak, *Konya, Central Anatolia*
early 19th century
Yataks are so called after the Turkish word for 'bed', for which they were used. This example has the traditional deep pile, which gives it its somewhat shaggy appearance (see also *Stripes*, *Plate 9*). Three rows of three archaic looking 'Memling' *güls* appear within white octagons on a glossy 'burnt' orange ground. Smaller star-filled octagons, which also appear at the 'Memling' *güls*' centres, are dispersed throughout the field. Stars appear within octagons in countless weaving traditions (for example, *Stars, Plates 3 and 8; and Border and Guard Patterns, Plate 2).*

15

16

17

Octagons and Güls

18 Yomut main carpet fragment, Turkmenistan (detail)

19th century

Kepse güls are made up of five jagged-edged vertical bands in alternating colours around an elongated octagon, with *ashik* (see *Abstract Shapes and Symbols, Plate 24*) motifs fitted on either side. Within each band anchor-shaped shrubs grow. 'C' shapes, not unlike those in *Plate 21* form pincers protruding into the field.

19 Yomut main carpet, Turkmenistan (detail)

19th century

The *dyrnak gül* takes its name from the Turkish word for claw ('tirnak'), obviously a reference to the hooks that characterize the ornament. Note how the colours used on the *güls* in each diagonal alternate. There are similarities between these ornaments and the hooked diamonds of *Abstract Shapes and Symbols, Plate 22,* these latter being considerably simpler in design and bolder in colour. On both examples hourglass filled diamonds form the centre of these ornaments. Here, 'T' shapes appear at each of the *gül's* points.

20 Chodor main carpet, Turkmenistan (detail)

19th century

The so-called *ertmen gül* is the primary motif of carpets and bags woven by the Chodor tribe. Here, they are not unlike small scalloped niches reflected through the horizontal axis. Diagonals of *ertmen güls* in red and white are alternated throughout the maroon field,

on which they appear to float like water lilies. Each ornament is filled with a column of three *ashiks* (see *Abstract Shapes and Symbols, Plate 24*).

21 Yomut main carpet, Turkmenistan (detail)

19th century

So-called 'C'-*güls,* also known as 'Moon' güls, are arranged in offset diagonal rows by means of three different colours (see *Figurative Motifs and Patterns, Plate 14; Stars, Plate 7;* and *Abstract Shapes and Symbols, Plate 24*). Sickle-like 'C' shapes fill both the outer and inner layer of these elongated octagonal *güls.* These shapes pervade Asian textile arts, especially Caucasian and early Anatolian rugs. The diamonds of *Abstract Shapes and Symbols, Plate 25,* which resemble *güls* in a number of ways, are filled with sets of four such 'C' shapes interlinked. The *güls* shown here have a high definition, achieved by an outline of a single row of knots in a contrasting colour, an effect often used on pilewoven pieces, such as, again, *Abstract Shapes and Symbols, Plate 25.*

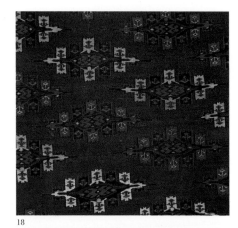

18

19

20

21

Border and Guard Patterns

Borders and guards are an important feature of textile art, and an idiosyncratic source of patterns. Usually the border comprises a middle band (the main border), with one or more 'guards' (also known as minor borders) on either side. These in turn are sometimes framed by thin stripes known as 'guard stripes'. Borders are patterned frames. They are to the field what guards are to a border: they highlight a pattern, ideally without overwhelming it, but also add a further design element to the whole.

Border designs serve a very different purpose to field designs. It is therefore unsurprising that border designs should often contrast sharply with those used in a field. So, the kufesque border in *Plates 1, 2* and *3*, could clearly not be employed in a field wholesale; similarly, trefoils (*Plates 17* and *18)* and samovars (*Plates 10* and *13*) tend to be found only in borders, unless the weaver is being innovative.

Sometimes, however, borders directly reflect a design found in a field; so, the two types of palmettes seen in *Plate 6* may be found in field designs elsewhere. The 'tile' border most frequently found on Mujur rugs appears also in the field of the so-called 'Chessboard' rugs, possibly from Damascus, of the 17th century (for example, *Compartments and Lattices, Plate 5*). A border can also pick up on a feature in the field. In *Plate 16*, peonies appear in both field and central border.

The width of borders can vary enormously, with a weaver sometimes utilising a 'vestigial' field to good effect, as in *Plate 9*. Here, the border encroaches on the field to such an extent that it becomes a focal point. Many kilims, on the other hand, use a very narrow border (e.g. *Plate 18*), or dispense with one altogether; striped flatweaves, from both old and new world, frequently have no borders (*Stripes, Plates 1* and *4*). A number of textiles also have no border.

Nowhere is the conservative nature of so many weaving cultures more apparent than in border designs. Often a particular group favoured one type of border, which they would employ consistently to frame a number of varying fields. Thus, a border is an important indicator of origin. The border in *Plate 5* is peculiar to Talish rugs from the southernmost Caucasus. The samovar border in *Plate 13* is commonly found on a variety of urban and village weavings from Northwest Persia. Whatever the information a border contains, however, it is significant that so many disparate traditions from so many different periods should favour the use of such a device.

1 *The Eskenazi early Anatolian carpet (detail)*
Seljuk period, 12th-14th century
The dramatic kufesque border is first found on what are thought to be Seljuk carpets (for the Seljuks, see *Abstract Shapes and Symbols, Plate 23*); its design appears to be a decorative rendition of 'Kufic' script, the earliest extant Islamic style of handwriting; it was used on the oldest known versions of the Qur'an, which date from the 8th to the 10th century.

2 *'Armorial' carpet fragment, Spain (detail)*
early 15th century
Numerous strips of different widths constitute a border; they are woven in knotted pile, but have the appearance of brocades. Their ornamentation includes: octagons filled with stars (see also *Stars, Plates 3* and *8*; *Octagons and Güls, Plate 17*), flowerheads, crosses and zoomorphic forms; zigzag chevrons; a chain of six-pointed stars outlined in blue and white; diagonal rows of diamonds like those on Anatolian brocades (see the diamonds in *Abstract Shapes ands Symbols, Plates 8* and *21*); and, most interestingly, a kufesque border like that in *Plate 1*, but perhaps farther removed from the original script. 'Armorial' carpets are so-called after the coats of arms which appear in the fields of those which survive intact.

3 *'Small Pattern Holbein' carpet, West Anatolia (detail)*
15th century
These carpets (see *Medallions, Plate 16*) often have kufesque borders. These lack some of the power seen in *Plates 2* and *3*, but are no less complex. On this example angular Kufic forms interlace and contain bold 'X' shapes in green or orange. Note also the flower-like 'C' shapes woven in the outer guard; these resemble the 'C' shapes found in *Abstract Shapes and Symbols, Plate 25* and *Octagons and Güls, Plate 18*.

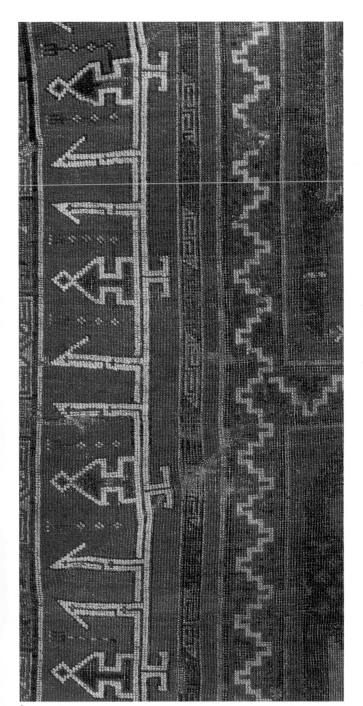

1

2

3

Border and Guard Patterns

4 Konya rug, Central Anatolia (detail)

late 18th century
Rounded simplified rosettes in red, blue and brown are joined by rectilinear vines or tendrils, which in turn suggest cartouche shapes.

5 Talish rug, Southern Caucasus (detail)

19th century
The 'rosettes' on this gleaming white border are typical of the elegant long rugs of Talish (see *Stars, Plate 7*) and indeed appear on few other borders. Their design dates back some 6,000 years, and is thought by some to represent inward-pointing arrows (see *Niches, Plate 6*). It seems that the weavers of Talish interpreted it as a rosette, setting it among groups of four small stylised flowerheads, with pairs of triangles for leaves. The motif itself appears as a field ornament on a number of rugs of different traditions (for example, on *Plate 9* and *Medallions, Plate 24*). Note also the reciprocal outer guard; these 'pawn' shapes are a simplified version of the trefoil border (see *Plate 17*).

6 Khorasan carpet, Northeast Persia (detail)

late 17th or early 18th century
Large jagged-edged palmettes chiefly woven in sea-green, blue, yellow and white alternate in direction on light madder. They are very similar to those used on *Palmettes, Plates 2* and *3*, and are separated by simpler palmettes like those in *Palmettes, Plate 5* in 'five-on-a-die' configuration.

Simple shrubs appear within the calyces of the larger palmettes.

7 Karabagh rug, South Caucasus (detail)

18th century
This border is comprised of palmettes which resemble samovars without handles (see also *Plate 13*) and saw-leaved, walnut coloured trees. These and other floriate motifs are set on a glowing yellow. Note also the *soldat* or 'tuning fork' pattern of the minor guards; the trunks of the stylised trees of *Trees and Leaves, Plate 33* are similarly decorated.

8 West Anatolian rug (detail)

16th/17th century
The 'leaf and wineglass' border is also found on numerous 19th century Caucasian rugs. Its clarity and simplicity, enhanced by the natural white on which the design is usually set, makes it an effective frame for many different field patterns.

9 Konya rug, central Anatolia (detail)

early 19th century
Sometimes the border is the main feature of a rug. Here the orange border, filled with outlandish stylised palmettes and angular abstract shapes, eclipses the darker vestigial field, which contains Talish-style rosettes (see *Plate 5*). One can also read the main 'border' as a field and the 'field' as a medallion.

4

5

6

7

8

9

Border and Guard Patterns

10 Transylvanian rug, West Anatolia (detail)

17th century

Polygonal cartouches filled with samovars (see also *Plate 13*) often embellish the border of so-called 'Transylvanian' rugs (see also *Medallions, Plate 10*). The older examples of the border alternate these cartouches with eight-pointed stars, as here. Note also the reciprocal trefoil guards (see *Plate 17*).

11 Mughal carpet, Lahore (?), Northwest India (detail)

early 17th century

Red octofoils, symmetrical fawn cartouches with blue cloudbands, and larger asymmetrical cartouches appear uniformly throughout this border. Further cartouches and roundels are cropped by the minor borders. A simpler rendition of a 'Classical' cartouche border is found on the 'Ardabil' carpet (*Medallions, Plate 2*).

12 Empire Aubusson pile carpet, France (detail)

c.1810

These cartouches are simple lozenges with eight-petalled flowers at their centre. The pink border of which they are part contains scrolling devices, very much in the Neo-Classical style, and brings to mind the patterns used in marquetry and rood-screens. The second border contains similar elements and is framed by guards of realistically drawn bouquets.

13 Ziegler carpet, Sultanabad (detail)

c.1880

The Manchester-based firm of Ziegler and Co. was the first (known) to organise the production and export of oriental carpets in Iran using Western capital; as such these carpets exemplify the Western perception of Persian designs. This border has been employed to frame numerous Northwest Persian decorative carpets. It is often referred to as the samovar border, after the shape of its palmette-filled principal motifs. Alternatively, it is called the 'tosbagheh' border, the Persian for 'turtle', which again these major ornaments resemble. These are alternated with elegant green serrated leaves curling round orange and blue flowerheads.

14 Mujur prayer rug, Central Anatolia (detail)

early 19th century

Mujur rugs are often identified by their border, whose design appears to derive from so-called 'Chessboard' rugs. The border elements are not dissimilar to the 'tiles' of one of these (*Compartments and Lattices, Plate 5*), each made up of a square filled with stars and complex triangular corners.

15 West Anatolian rug (detail)

18th century

Eight-pointed stars and 'hash' symbols are joined by an angular creeper on a dark brown ground. The border was to be adopted by later Caucasian traditions. It is appropriated in part by *Medallions, Plate 23*, where the stars have become greatly simplified, and the 'hash' symbol has been replaced by a fork-like motif.

10

11

12

13

14

15

Border and Guard Patterns

16 *Chinese velvet (detail)*
18th century
These borders have been executed with great precision on a deep orange. The inner border contains two systems of angular vines one in green, one in light blue; these end in points reminiscent of some elements of kufesque borders, which are known to have pervaded the Far East. The second border is an elaborate version of the peony border found on many Far Eastern carpets. The sprays joining each peony resemble cloudbands. The outer border is perhaps the most powerful of the three; it contains 'swastika' elements set within a labyrinth. Singularly Chinese in feel, a variant of this labyrinth pattern is found within the medallion of *Medallions, Plate 19*. One may also compare it with the borders seen in *Figurative Motifs and Patterns, Plate 4*.

17 *Yarkand long rug, East Turkestan (detail)*
18th century
Numerous versions of the reciprocal trefoil border appear throughout textile art (see *Plate 10*; *Abstract Shapes and Symbols, Plate 1*), but few can be as powerful and engaging as those found on carpets of East Turkestan. These trefoils are angular and cruciform, acquiring a certain grandeur from the red-gold colour combination. The East Turkestan examples are thought to derive from the 'Argali horn motif' found on Scythian felt work.

18 *Quashqa'i kilim, Southwest Persia (detail)*
19th century
The stepped reciprocal trefoil border commonly frames the simple patterns of tribal kilims of southern Persia (see *Compartments and Lattices, Plate 7*). Although the concept of the design is very simple, great strength is attained from the contrast between the dark blue and white.

19 *Salor* ensi, *Turkmenistan*
18th century
Octagons are not commonly found as border decorations. Here they alternate in dark blue and scarlet, each filled with groups of four two-tone stars. Note also the 'curled leaf' inner guard, which is also used as the border in *Palmettes, Plate 17* and *Figurative Motifs and Patterns, Plate 16* and (for the 'curled leaf', see *Trees and Leaves, Plate 4*). The clarity of design and precision in the layout of these borders are peerless.

16

17

18

19

Glossary

abrash – from the Turkish word *abraş*, meaning 'speckled' or 'piebald', this describes the variation in hue or colour found on many pile weavings, particularly those woven by nomads. This comes about either through subtle variations in colour due to the inconsistent dyeing of one wool batch, or through the introduction of a new wool batch while weaving a carpet. The former results in a gentle variegation throughout the field, the latter in a more dramatic change of hue or even colour. The effect can be quite attractive.

aksu – from the Turkish word for 'white water' or 'stream', a design found chiefly on Turkmen torbas, composed of a lattice of rectilinear brackets framing offset rows of abstract ornaments with protruding pincer shapes. See *Compartments and Lattices, Plate 13*.

appliqué – the surface decoration of a fabric, created by sewing, embroidering, or otherwise attaching to the ground cut-out, shapes. The crescents and tulips of *Palmettes, Plate 12*, for example, have been sewn onto the garment, and are not actually a part of the weave of the garment.

arabesques – literally, 'in the manner of Arabian designs', the arabesque consists primarily of split-leaf palmettes and other forms of stylised foliage connected by spiralling or undulating stems. Arabesques are characterised by a series of ornaments which intertwine, and are perhaps foliate in origin. See *Trees and Leaves, Plates 15-19*.

ashik – a simple ornament found primarily on Turkmen pieces (e.g. *Abstract Shapes and Symbols, Plate 24*), but appearing also on other Asian pileweaves (e.g. *Abstract Shapes and Symbols, Plate 25*). Symmetrical along the vertical axis, it is like a diamond with serrated edges. The ornament takes its name from '*aşik*', the Turkish word for knuckle-bones used in oracles and gaming.

asmalyk – from '*asma*', the Turkish for 'suspended, hanging', this is a pentagonal flank hanging, made to decorate camels for Turkmen wedding processions. See *Figurative Motifs and Patterns, Plate 3*.

ayna-khamtos – from '*ayna*' the Turkish for 'mirror' and '*khamtos*', the Turkmenian for 'stepped', this design comprises rows of rectangles, each filled with stepped diamonds. See *Compartments and Lattices, Plate 6*.

Bellini/re-entrant – a group of mainly Turkish rugs woven and exported to Italy in the 15th and first half of the 16th century. They are often woven in a prayer format with a niche at the top and a 'keyhole' shape pushing up into the field from the lower border, although the 'double-re-entrant' variant dispenses with the niche and uses two 'keyholes' at the top and base. The group are named after the Venetian painter, Gentile Bellini (?1429–1507), in whose paintings a number of rugs with this format appear. See *Niches, Plates 5–8* for examples.

bid majnun – the *bid majnun*, or weeping willow, design comprises the willow, cypress, poplar and fruit trees. Probably originally a Kurdish design (the earliest known examples are from Bijar, where Kurdish people are numerous), it has been copied in numerous weaving centres, testimony to its success as a pattern. See *Trees and Leaves, Plate 31*.

Bijov – a rectilinear pattern, composed of vertically connected palmettes (some like 'shields' – see *Palmettes, Plate 17*) flanked by split-leaf palmettes forming a central column, with columns of smaller floriate motifs on either side. See *Palmettes, Plate 16*.

bohça – the Turkish for 'bundle' or 'parcel', this term is used to describe an embroidered container for a Turkish bride's trousseau. See *Flowers, Plate 6*.

border – the frame of a carpet or textile, standardly comprising a middle band (the main border), with one or more 'guards' (also known as minor borders) on either side. There are many different permutations of border: sometimes just one narrow border, sometimes a 'guard' on one side and not the other, and so on. 'Border' is often used to describe simply the main border. See the chapter on *Border and Guard Patterns*.

boteh – the Persian for 'cluster of leaves', the *boteh* has been compared to the pine-cone, the almond, the pear, and even the Sacred Flame of Zoroaster. It is also said to be the shape brought about by the imprint of a closed fist on a mud or plaster surface. Few patterns can be as varied and widespread as those with repeating *botehs*; they appear on numerous pile- and flatweaves, especially from Western Iran and Central Asia. The design appears to have served as the inspiration for shawls made in Kerman in southern Iran, in Kashmir, India, and in Paisley in Scotland. See *Trees and Leaves, Plates 9–14*.

brocade – a vague term, used to refer to a variety of patterning techniques usually employing supplementary wefts. Sometimes wefts are introduced to form the pattern on a plain-weave ground, or it can be a weave, like a basket weave, in which warp and weft are passed over and under each other equally. It is these wefts which form the resulting pattern. See also *sumakh* and weft-wrapping. On *Palmettes, Plate 14*, silver thread is passed over a velvet ground to form a 'brocade'.

carpet – term often used to refer to room-sized woven pile pieces, and in England contrasted with the smaller 'rug'. In America 'rug' and 'carpet' are often interchangeable, although the largest pieces are always referred to as 'carpets'. See also *rug*.

cartouche – an ornament repeated throughout the border, or less frequently in the field, 'cartouche' usually signifies an ornate frame for a variety of motifs. See *Border and Guard Patterns, Plate 11*, for two types of cartouche.

chuval – tent bag. In Turkmen weavings, the term usually refers to the larger sizes of bag.

çintamani – typically comprising three dots placed over a pair of wavy lines, which resemble both lips and tiger stripes. It is said to take its name from a Buddhist ornament and can be traced back to textiles of the 10th century. Timur, the renowned conqueror commonly known as Tamerlane (1336–1405), adopted the design as an emblem in the 14th century. In 17th-century Turkey it was sometimes known as the 'leopard design'. The ornament goes back to antiquity; for example, three dots appear (without the wavy lines) as a vine on a vase painting attributed to the Greek settlement at Klozomenai on the Anatolian mainland in the 6th century BC. See *Abstract Shapes and Symbols, Plates 17–19*.

classical – a vague term used to refer to pre-19th-century court and workshop carpets

cloudband – a stylised depiction of a cloud which is often symmetrical and which resembles a band knotted at its collar (other cloud motifs are so described by extension). In its many manifestations, it spans the whole of Asia. See *Abstract Shapes and Symbols, Plates 1–6*.

elibelinde – an abstract motif, see *Abstract Shapes and Symbols, Plate 35*.

embroidery – the use of a variety of different needle-worked stitches to decorate fabrics.

ensi – Turkmen 'door' rugs, used to hang over the entrance of the 'yurt' (tent). *Ensis* usually have a specific compartment layout which perhaps suggests a wooden panelled door.

fēng-huang – the Chinese phoenix, adopted by several weaving traditions. See the phoenixes of *Figurative Motifs and Patterns, Plate 2*.

filikli – a non-Turkish word for the female goat, also used for weavings with angora knotted locks of up to 30cm.

fineness of weave – usually calculated in knots per sq. inch or sq. dm; the finer the weave, the greater the opportunity for precision and careful delineation.

fleur-de-lis – originally an iris flower, more usually associated with the former royal arms of France, these form part of many floral designs. See *Flowers, Plate 8*.

gol farang – a particular occidentalising style of flowerhead, perhaps the rose, frequently found on Persian rugs (e.g. *Flowers, Plate 15*). 'Farang' literally means 'from France', but came to denote 'European'.

guard – also known as the 'minor borders', these are the decorated bands which surround and enhance the main border.

guard stripe – thin stripes used to highlight guards and to separate them from the beginning of the field. Some very old weavings dispense with guard stripes altogether.

gül – for the sake of simplicity, the word 'gül' has been used throughout to describe a number of Turkmen ornaments arranged in endless repeat. Strictly speaking, however, this is inaccurate. A similar word 'göl' should be used to describe the primary ornaments on Turkmen main carpets, which are often regarded as tribal emblems; this word has not been used in this book. Instead, *gül* (from the Turkish word for 'rose', and the Persian word for 'flower'), which is correctly used to refer to all other Turkmen ornaments, has been used as a blanket term to cover both types of decoration. *Güls* are often an important indicator of tribal origin of a particular weaving. Specific varieties include *chemche, dyrnak, ertman, kepse,* Memling and *tauk nuska*; see *Octagons and Güls, Plates 6, 19, 20, 18, 15-17* and *6* respectively.

harshang – this rectilinear design takes its Persian name from its primary motif, a palmette which resembles a crab. A repeating pattern perhaps of Indian origin, it also displays clear stylistic connections with Safavid carpets. See *Palmettes, Plate 4*.

herati – this refers to a design used on a variety of carpets from Persia. Usually four *'fish heads'* or leaves are woven around a well-defined diamond, although this is sometimes omitted. At the same time, these motifs curl around a rosette. The design takes its name from Herat, now in Afghanistan, which had been for a long period the capital of Khorassan province in northeastern Iran. See *Trees and Leaves, Plate 8*.

interlace – the term used to describe interweaving within elements of a pattern. See, for example, how the stars within the 'endless knots' of *Medallions, Plate 16* are created by two crosses, in white and yellow, interlacing.

jajim – closely woven, striped textiles made up of a number of narrow joined strips of between 15 and 30cm in width. Sometimes decorated with brocade, these are utilitarian nomadic items put to a variety of uses. By some they are used as rugs, by others as mats or covers for sleeping on. See *Stripes, Plate 7*.

Joshaquani – a design of lozenges or tiles repeated over the whole of a field, each lozenge filled with flora or tree forms (like the 'weeping willow'). The pattern takes its name from Joshaquan, a town in central Persia, where carpets with such formats were made. See *Compartments and Lattices, Plate 14*.

kapunuk – from the Turkish, *kapı, kapu,* meaning 'door' or 'gate', this is a large mainly Turkmen weaving, shaped like the Greek letter 'pi', used as a door surround. See *Trees and Leaves, Plate 4*.

kesi – a term used to describe Chinese textiles woven in the slit-tapestry technique. See *Figurative Motifs and Patterns, Plate 24*.

kilim – Turkish for pileless carpet (in Persian '*gelim*'), the word is used universally to describe 'flatwoven' or 'plainwoven' textiles, in which the pattern is usually formed by the wefts alone ('weft-faced'), under which the warps are concealed. Though often woven in slit-tapestry, other techniques are also used. Plainweave may be 'weft-faced', 'warp-faced', or 'balanced' (i.e. when the pattern is formed by both warp and weft). See also *tapestry*.

kufesque – a border design which appears to be a decorative rendition of 'Kufic' script. This is the earliest extant Islamic style of handwriting and was used on the oldest known versions of the Qur'an, which date from the 8th to the 10th century. See *Border and Guard Patterns, Plates 1-3*.

lampas – an ill-defined type of brocade, not usually associated with any particular technique, so much as with the fabrics used and the overall appearance. See *Figurative Motifs and Patterns, Plate 11*.

lobe – a rounded division frequently found in medallions and in border ornaments.

lozenge – a diamond-shaped parallelogram or rhombus.

mihrab – from the Arabic for 'praying-place', a niche or slab used in mosques to indicate the direction of Mecca. 'Prayer' rugs utilise this form in their field.

'Mina Khani' – apocryphally thought to have been named after a man from Tabriz in northwest Persia, who devised the design. It is more likely to have originated among the weavers of western Persia, on whose weavings charming versions of the pattern appear. Generally the pattern comprises two types of major flowerheads, one daisy-like and set at the intersections of a trellis, the other more ragged and stylised, set within each compartment. See *Flowers, Plates 21 and 22*.

octofoil – round symmetrical ornaments with lobes or points in eight directions.

okbash – holder for tent-poles carried by Turkmen tribes in wedding caravans and during migration. See *Stripes, Plate 11*.

parmakli – the Turkish for 'finger', this refers to a particular type of design comprising rows or columns of comb-like elements, which when place together create further comb-like elements. The *parmakli* design appears on both Anatolian and Caucasian kilims. See *Abstract Shapes and Symbols, Plate 37*.

pileweave – the term used to refer to the structure of knotted pile carpets and rugs. Wool, silk or sometimes cotton are 'knotted' around a pair of warps in a variety of techniques, depending on the weaving tradition producing the carpet. The pile is the visible and tactile part of a carpet. See also *fineness of weave*.

P'u-lo – a design, found on the northwest frontier areas of China, of repeating dots. Each dot contains a further dot, a quality which has led some to believe that the design derives from Tibetan tie-dyed textiles. See *Abstract Shapes and Symbols, Plate 15*.

quatrefoil – round symmetrical ornaments with four lobes.

Re-entrant – see *Bellini*.

rug – in England, a pilewoven weaving of no more than about 40 sq. ft., in America the term is used for all but the largest of carpets. See also *carpet*.

saf – a prayer carpet, comprising multiple rows and/or columns of niches. See *Niches, Plate 1*.

samovar – the name sometimes given to a border ornament commonly used on northwest Persian carpets, but appearing on numerous weavings, resembling, as the name suggests, an urn. It is also referred to as the *tosbagheh*, the Persian for 'turtle', which these ornaments are also thought to resemble. See *Border and Guard Patterns, Plate 13*.

Shah Abbasi – the name given to numerous curvilinear Persian motifs of the Safavid period, after Shah Abbas (r. 1588–1629) who is known to have set up a court factory in his new capital, Esfahan. They include palmettes, cloudbands, vases, curled leaves, and so on, all usually connected by scrolling vines or a lattice, although they also appear with a medallion and corner format. Many 19th- and early 20th-century urban carpets hark back to the 'classical' period, and contain motifs which are described as 'Shah Abbasi' in the carpet trade. See *Palmettes, Plate 2*.

sileh – Caucasian utilitarian covers, usually in plainweave. See *Figurative Motifs and Patterns, Plate 8*.

slit-tapestry – the technique most commonly used on kilims, by which the patterning wefts turn back at the meeting of different colour areas. It is easily recognised by the small gaps appearing where there are colour changes. See also *kesi*.

Smyrna design – a design of multi-layered addorsed palmettes, reminiscent of acanthus leaves on 'Corinthian' column capitals. See *Palmettes, Plate 7*.

soldat – a Turkmen design often found in guard-stripes of repeating interlocking 'tuning-forks'. See *Trees and Leaves, Plate 33*.

spandrels – the 'corners' of a medallion and corner format carpet. These often correspond in design and size to one quarter of the central medallion, and are always intersected by the border.

strapwork – interlacing ornamentation imitating or resembling straps.

sumakh – a brocading technique. Wefts are 'wrapped' around the warp, usually passing over four warps, under two, over four again and so on. The *sumakh* techinque produces a clearly defined rectilinear pattern; only one set of wefts is used for the pattern, so strictly speaking they are not 'supplementary'. See *Figurative Motifs and Patterns, Plate 8*.

suzani – the word, derived from 'susan' (the Persian for 'needle'), used to describe a group of striking Central Asian embroideries on a cotton, or sometimes silk ground. Used as covers, they usually comprise stylised floral forms. See *Flowers, Plate 16*.

tapestry – a word used in a variety of ways. It refers to a specific technique or to this technique only when applied to pictorial patterning, or to such patterning when it is perceived as mural decoration. Sometimes it is used simply as 'wall-hanging'. Broadly speaking the technique is that of kilims, a plainweave that is 'weft-faced', 'warp-faced', or 'balanced'. 'Tapestry' can also be used as a generic term to describe numerous European pictorial weavings made in this way.

textile – 'textile' has two distinct meanings. Firstly, it is used as a generic term to describe any woven fabric. Usually, however, it is contrasted with pileweave and refers to embroideries, brocades, painted woven fabrics, flatweaves and pieces of other techniques.

torba – a tent bag used by Turkmen tribes for storage.

tosbagheh – see *samovar*.

trefoil – a clover-like ornament, comprising three lobes, often used in borders and guards, and valued for its reciprocal qualities. See *Border and Guard Patterns, Plates 17 and 18*.

warp – the vertical threads of a weaving as it is woven on the loom.

weft – threads intertwined at right angles with the warps. On kilims these usually constitute the pattern. On rugs and carpets, wefts are used (often in twos or threes) to hold the knots of the design in place.

weft-wrapping – see *brocade* and *sumakh*.

yastik – the Turkish word used to refer to weavings used as pillows or cushions. See *Medallions, Plate 15*.

yatak – from the Turkish word for 'bed', a *yatak* is a thickly piled Turkish weaving used to sleep on. See *Octagons and Güls, Plate 17*.

Yün Tsai T'ou – comprising so-called *j'ui* medallions, made up of four horn-shaped brackets, in a repeating pattern. The pattern is found only on weavings from China and East Turkestan. See *Compartments and Lattices, Plate 12*.

Further Reading

The literature on this subject is vast and therefore the following list is of necessity highly selective.

GENERAL INTRODUCTIONS TO CARPETS AND TEXTILES

Black, D. (ed.), *World Rugs and Carpets*, London 1985. A good introduction with essays by leading authorities. Edited by a stalwart of the London rug trade.

HALI – The International Magazine of Carpet and Textile Art. Published every two months in London, this is an indispensable tool for anyone wishing to get to grips with rugs and textiles. Numerous pictures and advertisements which present textiles as art. Outstanding colour reproduction.

Harris, J. (ed.), *5000 Years of Textiles*, London 1993. As comprehensive a selection of essays on textiles as you will find. Up-to-date and scholarly.

Opie, J., *Tribal Rugs*, London 1992. A thorough examination of the weavings of the nomadic peoples of Iran, Afghanistan, Turkey, the Caucasus and Central Asia, with lovely large illustrations and accurate colour reproduction. Some analysis of common patterns.

Thompson, J., *Carpets from the Tents, Cottages and Workshops of Asia*, London 1983. The most accessible survey of carpets to date, with intelligent comment and excellent examples.

PATTERNS
Carpets

Ford, P.R.J., *Oriental Carpet Design – A Guide to Traditional Motifs, Patterns and Symbols*, London 1981. Bestseller for beginners with over 800 illustrations of varying quality.

Gantzhorn, V. , *The Christian Oriental Carpets – Its Development, Iconologically and Iconographically, from its Beginnings to the 18th century*. Cologne 1991. A tendentious work tracing carpet patterns back to Phrygian and other traditions in over 500 pages. With varied and beautiful illustrations including book illuminations, paintings and architectural details. A wonderful document of archaic designs.

Klieber, H., *Turkestan*, Landsberg 1991. An ethnographic account containing a near-comprehensive exegesis of Turkmen carpet ornaments with line drawings.

Loges, W., *Turkoman Tribal Rugs*, London, 1980. The seminal account of every variety of Turkoman weaving. Accessible.

Pinner, R., *The Rickmers Collection – Turkoman Rugs*, London 1993. Catalogue of a collection donated to the Museum of Ethnography, Berlin. Good colour and clear text with a useful glossary and line drawings. A good introduction to those who wish to pursue Turkmen weavings further.

Schurmann, U., *Caucasian Carpets*, Cologne 1964. A long-lasting account from the foremost rug dealer of the postwar period. Concentrating on the weavings of the 19th century, the book provides a clear, if factually dubious, taxonomy.

Turkish Handwoven Carpets, vols. I-V, Ankara 1990–95. A very good pictorial overview of Turkish pile weavings from the 13th to the 20th centuries still in their country of origin. Includes some of the most impressive known examples of early Turkish weaving. Poor on colour and detail. Published by the Turkish Ministry of Culture.

Textiles

Abegg, M., *Apropos Patterns For Embroidery, Lace and Woven Textiles*, Bern 1978. From the foremost centre for textile conservation in the world, a study of patterns and pattern books.

Beck, T., *The Embroiderer's Flowers*, Devon 1992. Examining the centuries-old use of flowers in embroidery. A good source book for Western floral designs.

Erber, C., *A Wealth of Silk and Velvet*. Catalogue from an exhibition of Ottoman textiles, focusing on velvets and embroideries from 15th to 18th centuries. Beautiful examples, well illustrated.

Gluckman, D.C., Hanyu, G. et al., *Heavens' Embroidered Cloths – One Thousand Years of Chinese Textiles*, Hong Kong 1995. Catalogue of a high-profile exhibition, containing well-reproduced illustrations of exemplary Chinese costumes and textiles.

Hale, A. and Fitzgibbon, K., with photographs by Doris Rau, *Ikats – Woven silks from Central Asia. The Rau Collection* , Oxford 1988. Good catalogue of a varied collection with bleed details that serve as useful pattern sources. Clear introduction to the subject.

Hanyu, G., *Chinese Textile Designs*, London 1992. Authoritative text with many large illustrations that give a good overview of Far Eastern motifs and patterns.

Klimberg, M., *Ikat – Textile Art from the Silk Road*, Vienna 1993. Beautifully produced book of an exhibition held at the Kirdök Gallery in Vienna. With over 80 colour plates of good examples.

Meller, S., *Textile Designs*, New York 1991. Over 400 pages of drawings, with each design carefully classified. Concentrating on European and American designs.

Parry, L., *William Morris Textiles*, London 1983. A good introduction to the designs of Morris, with a useful catalogue of printed textiles.

Reid, J.W., *Textile Art of Peru*, Peru 1989. Covering over 2,000 years of Peru's rich textile heritage, this book contains some of the finest examples known, culled from museums and private collections.

Rothstein, N., *Silk Designs of the Eighteenth Century in the Collection of the Victoria and Albert Museum, London*, London 1990. A complete catalogue of the collection of 18th century woven silk in the Victoria & Albert Museum with excellent colour illustrations. Includes an interesting section on the Museum's mid 18th-century pattern books.

Stone-Miller, R., *To Weave for the Sun*, Boston 1992. Catalogue of the impressive array of Andean textiles in the Museum of Fine Arts, Boston.

The Topkapi Saray Museum, translated, expanded and edited by J.M. Rogers, Boston and London 1986-88. A catalogue in five volumes of the holdings of the Topkapi Saray museum in Istanbul. Ottoman costumes and embroideries, textiles, albums and illustrated manuscripts, carpets and architecture. Contains spectacular examples.

The Victoria and Albert Museum British Textile Series, London 1992–94. With good, large, accurate colour illustrations, excellent object-led accounts of all aspects of Britain's textiles from 1200 to the beginning of this century.

Islamic Patterns

Hedgecoe, J. and Damluji, S., *Zillij – The Art of Moroccan Ceramics*, Reading 1992. A photographic record of Moroccan ceramics, with written contributions from leading art historians and architects. An excellent source for geometric Islamic patterns.

Kühnel, E., translated by Ettinghausen, R., *The Arabesque – Meaning and Transformation of an Ornament*, Graz 1976. Good account of a widespread and difficult to define ornament, translated from the 1949 German original by a respected Islamicist.

Wilson, E., *Islamic Designs*, London 1988. Clear drawings of designs from a variety of different media. One in a series of good source books called *British Museum Pattern Books* (also Early Medieval, North American Indian and Ancient Egyptian designs).

Other Patterns

Jones, O., *The Grammar of Ornament*, London 1986. Reprint of a Victorian classic. An account of world patterns from the Stone Age to 19th century that makes claims to be definitive and comprehensive. Dogmatic but rivetting.

The Thames and Hudson Celtic Design Series, London 1991–95. A series of short and accessible handbooks with good line drawings.

Wilson, E., *8,000 Years of Ornament – An Illustrated Handbook of Motifs*, London 1994. Analyses and explains the most important decorative motifs of many cultures from prehistory to the present day. Good line drawings.

Pattern Analysis

Christie, A.H., *Pattern Design An Introduction to the Study of Formal Ornament*, New York 1969. A good, if old-fashioned handbook analysing the evolution and structure of formal ornament

Critchlow, K., *Islamic Patterns – An Analytical and Cosmological Approach*, London 1989. For those who wish to delve deeper into the cosmological principles underlying many patterns.

El-Said, I., *The System of Geometric Design – Islamic Art and Architecture* Reading 1993. Pinpoints the geometric rules of composition. Two chapters from an important doctoral thesis, examining the underlying unity of all Islamic designs.

Washburn, D.K. and Crowe, D.W., *Symmetries of Culture – Theory and Practice of Plane Pattern Analysis*, Seattle & London 1988. A survey of symmetry in world cultures as a means for classification and identification. Important, interesting, and user friendly.

Picture Acknowledgements

The following abbreviations have been used:
AM: Collection of Alan Marcuson
Buccleuch: By kind permission of the Duke of Buccleuch/Photo: Longevity
CL: Christie's, London
CNY: Christie's, New York
HA: Hali Archive
RP: Richard Purdon, Oxfordshire
SNL: Sotheby's, London
SNY: Sotheby's, New York
TAP: T.A.P. Photo Library, London

Flowers:
1. SNY. 2. Metropolitan Museum of Art, New York, Bequest of Benjamin Altman, inv. no.14.40.723. 3. Collection A.E.D.T.A., Paris, inv. no. 1154. 4. HA. 5. CL. 6. Battilossi, Turin. 7. HA. 8. SNY. 9. Collection of the Biltmore Estate, Asheville, North Carolina. 10. SL. 11. RP. 12. AM. 13. CL. 14. SNY. 15. Daniele Sevi, Milan. 16. Esther Fitzgerald, London. 17. HA. 18. SNY. 19. CL. 20. SNY. 21. Private Collection, USA. 22. Private Collection, London. 23. Skinner, Inc., Auctioneers and Appraisers of Antiques and Fine Art, Boston.

Palmettes:
1. Buccleuch. 2. Buccleuch. 3. HA. 4. SNY. 5. SNY. 6. HA. 7. TAP. 8. SNY. 9. SL. 10. HA. 11. HA. 12. Topkapi Saray Museum, Istanbul, inv. no. 13/514. 13. HA. 14. HA. 15. HA. 16. Raoul Tschebull, Darien, Connecticut. 17. John Eskenazi, London. 18. SNY. 19. HA.

Trees and Leaves:
1. Davide Halevim Gallery, Milan. 2. David Black Oriental Carpets, London. 3. Rippon Boswell, Wiesbaden. 4. CNY. 5. CL. 6. TAP. 7. TAP. 8. HA. 9. HA. 10. HA. 11. Textile Museum, Washington, DC, Gift of Arthur D. Jenkins, 1961.39.6. 12. TAP. 13. Maison du Tapis d'Orient, Istanbul. 14. SNY. 15. SL. 16. Topkapi Saray Museum, Istanbul. 17. Buccleuch. 18. CL. 19. SL. 20. SL. 21. By kind permission of Edward Hulse, Breamore House. 22. Collection A.E.D.T.A., Paris, inv. no. 1272. 23. HA. 24. AM. 25. HA. 26. Samarkand Galleries, Gloucestershire. 27. HA. 28. SNY. 29. Tom Murray, Mill Valley, USA. 30. Private Collection, London. 31. RP. 32. AM. 33. AM.

Compartments and Lattices:
1. SL. 2. Private Collection, London. 3. AM. 4. Royal Collection Enterprises. 5. SNY. 6. Textile Museum, Washington, DC, Jenkins Collection, inv. no. 1980.13.8. 7. Rippon Boswell, Wiesbaden. 8. CL. 9. SNY. 10. John Eskenazi, London. 11. SNY. 12. CL. 13. AM. 14. CL. 15. AM. 16. Keir Collection, Richmond, Surrey. 17. CL. 18. Photo Library, London.

Medallions:
1. CL. 2. Victoria and Albert Museum, London, inv. no. 272-1893. 3. Buccleuch. 4. SNY. 5. RP. 6. Museum für Islamische Kunst, Berlin, inv. no. I.2577. 7. Buccleuch. 8. John Eskenazi, London. 9. Galerie Sailer, Salzburg. 10. AM. 11. Private Collection, Italy/ photo: Alberto Boralevi. 12. SNY. 13. Orient Stars Collection, Stuttgart. 14. SNY. 15. SL. 16. Courtesy of the Wher Collection, Switzerland. 17. HA. 18. TAP. 19. SNY. 20. The David Collection, Copenhagen. 21. Rippon Boswell, Wiesbaden. 22. Türk ve Islam Eserleri Müzesi, Istanbul. 23. AM. 24. James Opie. 25. SNY. 26. AM.

Niches:
1. Museum für Islamische Kunst, Berlin, inv. no. I.25/61. 2. The al-Sabah Collection, Dar al-Athar al-Islamiyyah, Kuwait. 3. Topkapi Saray, Museum, Istanbul, inv. no. 13/2042. 4. HA. 5. Museum für Islamische Kunst, Berlin, inv. no. I.88/30. 6. Topkapi Saray Museum, Istanbul, inv. no. 13/2043. 7. TAP. 8. Metropolitan Museum of Art, inv. no. 22.100.109. 9. Victoria and Albert Museum, London, inv. no. T312.1920. 10. HA/SNY. 11. HA. 12. CL. 13. SNY. 14. HA. 15. SL. 16. M.H. de Young Memorial Museum, The Fine Arts Museums of San Francisco, California. 17. CL. 18. Alex Sadeh, London.

Figurative Motifs and Patterns:
1. Parviz and Manijeh Tanavoli, Vancouver. 2. Shumei Family Collection, Shigaraki, Japan. 3. Peter Hoffmeister, Dörfles-Esbach, Germany. 4. SL. 5. Textile Museum, Washington, DC, 68.00.20A. 6. Skinner Inc., Auctioneers and Appraisers of Antiques and Fine Art. 7. SNY. 8. SNY. 9. Jeremy Pine, London. 10. CNY. 11. Spink and Son, London.

12. Vienna Angewandte Kunst. 13. Victoria and Albert Museum, London, inv. no. IS 34-1969/Horst Kolo. 14. Indianapolis Museum of Art, Indiana, The Boucher Collection. 15. Galerie Sailer, Salzburg, Austria. 16. Courtesy of the Wher Collection, Switzerland. 17. Linda Wrigglesworth, Chinese Costume and Textiles, London. 18. AM. 19. SNY. 20. AM. 21. SNY. 22. Paul Hughes Fine Textile Art, London. 23. Edward H. Merrin, New York. 24. Linda Wrigglesworth, Chinese Costume and Textiles, London. 25. AM. 26. SNY. 27. Museum für Islamische Kunst, Berlin, inv. no. I.4.

Stars:
1. Orient Stars Collection, Stuttgart. 2. Museum of Applied Arts, Budapest. 3. Museum für Islamische Kunst, Berlin. 4. AM. 5. CL. 6. The al-Sabah Collection, Dar al-Athar al-Islamiyyah, Kuwait. 7. HA. 8. AM. 9. Orient Star Collection, Stuttgart. 10. Private Collection, USA. 11. Private Collection, USA. 12. HA. 13. SNY. 14. HA.

Stripes:
1. CNY. 2. RP. 3. William Siegal Collection, Santa Fe. 4. HA. 5. RP. 6. HA. 7. Peter Willborg, Stockholm. 8. HA. 9. Udo Hirsch, Adenau, Germany. 10. Richard Purdon, Oxfordshire. 11. SNY. 12. RP. 13. RP. 14. AM. 15. RP.

Abstract Shapes and Symbols:
1. Victoria and Albert Museum, London, inv. no. 589.1890. 2. Museum für Islamische Kunst, Berlin, inv. no. I.24. 3. Rijksmuseum, Amsterdam, inv. no. RBK 17271. 4. Buccleuch. 5. HA. 6. AM. 7. Rippon Boswell, Wiesbaden. 8. AM. 9. SNY. 10. M.H. de Young Memorial Museum, The Fine Arts Museums of San Francisco, California. 11. AM. 12. RP. 13. Private Collection, Germany. 14. HA. 15. HA. 16. HA. 17. Textile Museum, Washington, DC, inv. no. 1976.10.1. 18. Vakiflar Carpet Museum, Istanbul. 19. Private Collection, Los Angeles. 20. AM. 21. AM. 22. AM. 23. Private Collection, Germany. 24. SL. 25. Pacific Northwest Collection. 26. Rippon Boswell, Wiesbaden. 27. SNY. 28. RP. 29. Private Collection, Cologne. 30. Galerie Sailer, Salzburg. 31. AM. 32. HA. 33. HA. 34. Dario Valcarenghi, Milan, Italy. 35. M.H. de Young Memorial Museum, The Fine Arts Museums of San Francisco, California. 36. Kailash Gallery, Antwerp. 37. M.H. de Young Memorial Museum, The Fine Arts Museums of San Francisco, California. 38. Finarte Casa d'Aste, Milan. 39. Musée Jacquemart-André, Paris, inv. no. 1019. 40. Parviz and Manijeh Tanavoli, Vancouver.

Octagons and Güls:
1. AM. 2. AM. 3. RP. 4. Anthony Thompson, London. 5. Orient Stars Collection, Stuttgart. 6. AM. 7. SNY. 8. SNY. 9. James Blackmon, San Francisco. 10. HA. 11. RP. 12. SL. 13. AM. 14. Orient Stars Collection, Stuttgart. 15. HA. 16. SNY. 17. HA. 18. AM. 19. AM. 20. AM. 21. AM.

Border and Guard Patterns:
1. Orient Stars Collection, Stuttgart. 2. Museum für Islamische Kunst, Berlin, inv. no. 79.363. 3. Finarte Casa d'Aste, Milan. 4. TAP. 5. SNY. 6. John Eskenazi, London. 7. HA. 8. TAP. 9. TAP. 10. TAP. 11. Buccleuch. 12. SNY. 13. David Black Oriental Carpets, London. 14. TAP. 15. TAP. 16. AM. 17. SNY. 18. Galerie Sailer, Salzburg. 19. Private Collection, London.

Index